MACMILLAN/McGRAW-HILL
INTEGRATED
LANGUAGE ARTS
ACTIVITY BOOK

GRADE 3

Grammar, Mechanics, and Usage Practice and Handbook
Glossary of Writing, Language, and Literary Terms
Writing Models and Prompts
Spelling Strategies and Tips

Printed on recycled paper.

MACMILLAN/McGRAW-HILL SCHOOL PUBLISHING COMPANY
New York   Columbus

D1444714

Macmillan/McGraw-Hill School Division
10 Union Square East
New York, New York 10003

Printed in the United States of America
ISBN 0-02-180461-3 / 3
1 2 3 4 5 6 7 8 9 BAW 99 98 97 96 95 94

TABLE OF CONTENTS

GRAMMAR, MECHANICS, AND USAGE PRACTICE

TABLE OF CONTENTS

Grammar, Mechanics, and Usage Handbook and Glossary

Writing Models

TABLE OF CONTENTS

Writing Prompts

Spelling Strategies

Cumulative Word List

What Is a Sentence?

A **sentence** is a group of words that tells a complete idea. It tells who is doing something or what is happening.

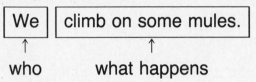

| We | | climb on some mules. |

↑   ↑

who   what happens

A sentence: The canyon is huge.
Not a sentence: An unusual sight.

A. Circle each group of words that is a sentence.

1. The mules climb slowly.

2. The guide leads the way.

3. Larger than all of Rhode Island.

4. The Colorado River formed the walls of the canyon.

5. Took many years.

6. We make our way down slowly.

7. The mules are sure-footed.

8. Many of the tourists.

B. Circle **yes** if the group of words forms a sentence. Circle **no** if they do not.

9. Thousands of tourists visit the Grand Canyon.   yes   no

10. Along the trails.   yes   no

11. Some people ride mules into the canyon.   yes   no

12. A long ride to the bottom.   yes   no

13. Others come in by raft on the Colorado River.   yes   no

14. The canyon is beautiful.   yes   no

15. Very popular vacation spot.   yes   no

What Is a Sentence?

A **sentence** is a group of words that tells a complete idea. It tells who is doing something or what is happening.

A sentence: Caves are interesting places.
Not a sentence: Want to explore one.

A. Read each group of words. Write **yes** if the words make a sentence. Write **no** if they do not.

1. The cave was very dark. _____

2. Mom used her flashlight. _____

3. Had one, too. _____

4. Entered first. _____

5. The rest of us followed. _____

6. The huge, dark cave. _____

7. Dad heard a noise in the distance. _____

8. Wondered what it was. _____

B. Write each group of words so that they form a sentence.

9. walked for a long time

_____

10. I heard a

_____

11. grew louder and louder

_____

12. left very quickly

_____

13. glad to be out

_____

Macmillan/McGraw-Hill

What Is a Sentence?

Vacation Memories

Carlo is putting some vacation photographs in a book. He has written about each one. He hasn't always written sentences, though. Help Carlo by drawing a line through each group of words that is not a sentence. Write each sentence on the line.

1. Dad and I collect shells.

Close to the water.

_____

3. Wings that are very wide!

A sea gull flies overhead.

_____

2. Mom and Felisa build a castle.

Grows taller and taller.

_____

_____

4. Mom and Dad on the beach.

Mom and Dad watch the sunset.

_____

_____

Statements and Questions

A **statement** is a sentence that tells something.

| We are going to China. | → statement |

| The plane is taking off. | → statement |

A **question** is a sentence that asks something.

| Will you visit the Great Wall? | → question |

| May I come along? | → question |

A. Tell whether the sentence is a statement or a question. Circle the correct word.

1. Is the Great Wall of China very long?   statement   question

2. It is the longest wall ever built.   statement   question

3. The wall was built by hand.   statement   question

4. It is more than 4,000 miles long.   statement   question

5. Was it made very long ago?   statement   question

6. The wall was started in the 400's B.C.   statement   question

7. Why did the Chinese build the wall?   statement   question

8. The wall was built for protection.   statement   question

9. It kept China's enemies out.   statement   question

B. Underline each sentence that is a statement. Circle each sentence that is a question.

10. Parts of the wall have crumbled.

11. Many sections have been repaired.

12. How tall is the wall?

13. Soldiers once marched along the wall.

Name _____

Statements and Questions

A **statement** is a sentence that tells something.
> Spelunking means exploring caves.

A **question** is a sentence that asks something.
> Have you ever gone spelunking?

A. Read each sentence. If it tells something, write **statement** next to it. If it asks something, write **question.**

1. Spelunking is a hobby. _____
2. Is spelunking hard to do? _____
3. Spelunkers go in groups. _____
4. Can they get hurt? _____
5. People often get lost in caves. _____
6. What kind of equipment is needed? _____

B. Rewrite each sentence correctly.

7. spelunkers need hard hats and lamps

_____

8. what else do they need

_____

9. is a compass necessary

_____

10. spelunkers carry ropes

_____

11. exploring caves is hard work

_____

Commands and Exclamations

Magic Number

Find the magic number. First, circle all the commands. Then, follow each command to find the magic number. You may write in the boxes below.

1. This is a great trick!

2. Get a pencil.

3. What a fun thing to show your friends!

4. Write a number from one through ten in the box.

5. Add six to that number.

6. Write the sum.

7. What a simple problem!

8. Subtract four from the sum.

9. How easy this is for you!

10. Next, add five to the difference.

11. Subtract the number you started with.

12. You have now found the magic number!

13. Start with a different number and follow the commands again.

Now complete this sentence.

The magic number is ____ .

Macmillan/McGraw-Hill

Mechanics: Punctuating Sentences

A **statement** and a **command** end with a period.

Statement: | I love the ocean. |

Command: | Dive into the ocean. |

A **question** ends with a question mark.

| Will you come along? |

An **exclamation** ends with an exclamation point.

| What a time we will have! |

Circle the correct end punctuation for each sentence.

1. Gather all your gear . ? !

2. Is your tank full . ? !

3. You can use my extra flippers . ? !

4. Gee, the water's freezing . ? !

5. Put on your wet suit . ? !

6. It is colder down below . ? !

7. Will we dive far . ? !

8. We'll go down about thirty feet . ? !

9. Wow, that's deep . ? !

10. Are you ready for the plunge . ? !

11. That creature to our left is a sea turtle . ? !

12. It's huge . ? !

13. Is it dangerous . ? !

14. No, it is just big . ? !

15. Take a picture of it . ? !

Mechanics: Punctuating Sentences

> A **statement** and a **command** end with a period.
>
> > **Statement:** We are leaving for outer space.
> > **Command:** Buckle your safety belts.
>
> A **question** ends with a question mark.
>
> > Are you ready for the journey?
>
> An **exclamation** ends with an exclamation point.
>
> > I can hardly wait!

A. Write whether each sentence is a **statement, question, command,** or an **exclamation.** Circle the end punctuation.

1. Mission Control says we can go. _____

2. Start the engines. _____

3. What a roar they make! _____

4. Can we lift off now? _____

5. The weather is perfect. _____

6. What a fine blast-off this is! _____

B. Write each sentence. Add the correct end punctuation.

7. We are now above the earth

_____

8. How peaceful it all seems

_____

9. You may undo your safety belts

_____

10. Can you see that planet

_____

Macmillan/McGraw-Hill

Mechanics: Punctuating
Sentences

Divide and Multiply!

Each group of words below is made up of two sentences. Working with a partner, draw a line between the two sentences. Then rewrite each one on the lines provided. Start each one with a capital letter and add the correct end punctuation.

1. you can grow a garden put carrot tops in water

_____

_____

2. do you have a sweet potato what a pretty vine it will grow

_____

_____

3. write a message on paper with lemon juice hold it near a light bulb

_____

_____

4. are tomatoes vegetables or fruits tomatoes are fruits

_____

_____

5. what plant has eyes a potato has eyes

_____

_____

6. we eat the roots of some plants what other parts do we eat

_____

_____

Capitalization and Punctuation of Compound Sentences

When you want to connect two sentences with similar ideas, join the sentences with *and.*

A sentence that contains two sentences joined by a **comma** and the words *and, or,* or *but* is called a **compound sentence**.

Always capitalize the first word of a sentence, and use the correct punctuation at the end of a sentence.

Join each pair of sentences. Use the word in ( ).

1. It was a hot day. (and)
Lisa and Bobby wanted to swim.

_____

2. They could swim at the beach. (or)
They could swim in the pool.

_____

3. They took their beach towels. (and)
Lisa called some friends.

_____

4. Bobby wanted to pack a lunch. (but)
He didn't have enough time.

_____

5. Bobby played volleyball with Tommy. (and)
Lisa played catch with Sharon.

_____

Macmillan/McGraw-Hill

Capitalization and Punctuation of Compound Sentences

A **compound sentence** contains two sentences joined by a comma and the words *and, or,* or *but.*

Compound sentences give you the opportunity to join two sentences with similar ideas.

Always **capitalize** the first word of a sentence and use the correct punctuation at the end of a sentence.

Join each pair of sentences. Use the word in ( ).

1. Our family visited a travel agent. (and)
We planned a vacation.

_____

2. Our flight was delayed for three hours. (but)
We were patient.

_____

3. I could sit in an aisle seat. (or)
I could sit in a window seat.

_____

4. Mother read a travel magazine. (but)
Dad looked out the window.

_____

5. The airplane food was bad. (and)
My little brother cried the whole time.

_____

Macmillan/McGraw-Hill

Capitalization and Punctuation of Compound Sentences

I Know You!

How much do you know about the people in your life? Write a sentence that tells two things about each person. If you don't have a relative on the list, a brother for example, you may want to write about someone else's brother. Remember to use *and, or,* or *but* to combine each sentence. Try to use each one at least once. The first one is given as an example.

1. your brother _____

_____

2. your neighbor _____

_____

3. your mother _____

_____

4. your teacher _____

_____

5. your grandmother _____

_____

6. your best friend _____

_____

Macmillan/McGraw-Hill

Capitalization and Punctuation of Names and Titles

Capitalize the names of people.

Brenda Kerr   **Howard Gold**

Capitalize words that show family relationships when used as titles or as substitutes for a person's name.

Uncle Frank will drive us to the game.

Capitalize titles of respect or titles when they come before the names of people.

Doctor Joi   **Señor** Rocha   **Professor** Bartowski

Rewrite the following using the correct capitalization and punctuation.

1. sharon Smith _____

2. captain davila _____

3. Mister kachur _____

4. carlos vega _____

5. president clinton _____

6. doctor young _____

7. general foley _____

8. cassandra _____

9. Mom and dad took us hiking.

_____

10. We are honoring lieutenant brown for his work on the police force.

_____

Capitalization and Punctuation of Names and Titles

Capitalize the names of people.
Lionel Morgan   **Manuel Sanchez**

Capitalize titles of respect or titles when they come before the names of people.
Judge Marlene Devaney   **Captain** Bill Bevich
Doctor Marisa Rodriguez

Capitalize words that show family relationships when used as titles or as substitutes for a person's name.
Ask **Mom** and **Uncle Elliot** what the movie is about.

Rewrite the following sentences using the correct capitalization and punctuation.

1. mary sent a birthday invitation to professor fred bonato.

_____

2. Fred is friendly with grandpa.

_____

3. She also invited uncle Scott and aunt Natalie.

_____

4. Mr. and Mrs. rivera would like to go to Grandpa's party.

_____

5. Uncle mark and grandmother will prepare all the food.

_____

6. Joseph and saul will provide the entertainment.

_____

Macmillan/McGraw-Hill

Capitalization and Punctuation of Names and Titles

Keep in Touch!

Conner wrote a letter to his friend Kelsey telling her about his new school. Help Conner fix the mistakes in his letter before he mails it. Circle all the errors. Then rewrite the letter correctly on the lines below.

Dear kelsey,

    How are you? I like my new school. The bus ride to school is very long, but the bus driver Mr. kresge is very funny. My teacher's name is Mrs. dombrosky. I was a little scared the first day, but she introduced me to the class, and I felt better. One girl named roxanne asked me a lot of questions about my old school. My next-door neighbors are very nice. One boy's name is tommy. He rides on the bus with me. His Brother helped mom and dad paint the house. mom said you should visit us this summer. I would like that. Please write back soon.

Your friend,
Conner

_____

_____

_____

_____

_____

_____

_____

_____

_____

_____

Macmillan/McGraw-Hill

Capitalization and Punctuation of Dates, Months, and Days of the Week

---

Capitalize the days of the week and the months of the year.

Sunday   **Wednesday**   **May**   **September**

When writing the date, use a **comma** between the day and the year.
September 7, 1995

Do not use a comma if only the month and the year are given.
June 1995

A. Decide whether each group of words is correct or incorrect.
Underline **yes** or **no**.

1. March 4, 1952   <u>yes</u>   no

2. January 2 1991   yes   <u>no</u>

3. April 6 1994   yes   <u>no</u>

4. January 1995   <u>yes</u>   no

B. Rewrite the following sentences using the correct capitalization
and punctuation.

5. We are visiting Acadia National Park on july 9, 1996.

_____

6. We will arrive on a saturday and return the following sunday.

_____

7. I like to go camping during august.

_____

8. Last year on July 14 1994, we visited the Grand Canyon.

_____

Macmillan/McGraw-Hill

Capitalization and Punctuation of Dates, Months, and Days of the Week

---

Capitalize the days of the week and months of the year.
Thursday   Saturday   October   January

When writing the date, use a comma between the day and the year.
February 14, 1995

Do not use a comma if only the month and the year are given.
April 1982

A. Rewrite the following sentences using the correct capitalization and punctuation.

1. On july 4 1776, the 13 colonies declared their independence.

_____

2. I was born on february 1 1985.

_____

3. Our vacation is planned for june, 1997.

_____

4. Franklin Roosevelt died on april 12 1945.

_____

B. Rewrite the following correctly on the line provided.

5. february   _____

6. june 6 1982   _____

7. march   _____

8. november   _____

9. December   _____

10. April, 1996   _____

Capitalization and Punctuation of Dates, Months, and Days of the Week

It's a Date!

Some people find it helpful to write down their weekly or monthly schedules in advance, to keep track of all their appointments and activities. Put some order in your life by writing down the days, the dates, and your daily plans for the next 15 days. Use the lines below to prepare your schedule.

_____

_____

_____

_____

_____

_____

_____

_____

_____

_____

_____

_____

_____

_____

Capitalization and Punctuation of Places, Addresses, and Historical Events

Use a **comma** between the name of a city and a state in an address. Use a **comma** before and after the name of a state or country when it is used with the name of a city in a sentence.

Tucson, Arizona

Some of my relatives live in **Detroit, Michigan,** and **Dallas, Texas,** but most live in **Los Angeles, California.**

Capitalize the names of cities, states, and countries.

Taos   **Idaho**   **Mexico**

Capitalize the names of streets and highways.

Market Street   **Highway 209**

Capitalize the names of historical events.

World War I   **Middle Ages**

Write the following words and groups of words using correct capitalization and punctuation.

1. egypt _____

2. yuma california _____

3. boston massachusetts _____

4. london lane _____

5. the great depression _____

6. midville avenue _____

7. newark new jersey _____

8. denver colorado _____

9. korean war _____

10. route 280 _____

Capitalization and Punctuation of Places, Addresses, and Historical Events

---

Capitalize
- names of cities (**Cleveland**), states (**South Dakota**), and countries (**China**)
- names of streets and highways (**Orchard Street, Route 46**)
- historical events (**the Boston Tea Party**)

Use a comma
- between city and state in an address
  Omaha, Nebraska
- before and after the state or country when it is used with the name of a city in a sentence
  The car ride to **Lubbock, Texas,** was very long.

Rewrite the following sentences using the correct capitalization and punctuation.

1. The civil war began in 1861.

_____

2. The first battle of the civil war took place in charleston, south carolina.

_____

3. One of the greatest Civil War battles took place at gettysburg pennsylvania.

_____

4. In 1865, General Lee surrendered to General Grant at appomattox, virginia.

_____

Capitalization and Punctuation of Places, Addresses, and Historical Events

A Former Capital

In each sentence, one proper noun is written incorrectly. Write it in the letter spaces with the correct capitalization and punctuation. The boxed letters will spell out the name of the mystery city that the sentences tell about.

1. This city is in the state of pennsylvania. □_ _ _ _ _ _ _ _ _ _

2. That state lies east of the state of Ohio. _□_ _

3. The city was founded by william penn. _□_□_ _ _ _ _ _

4. Ben Franklin moved there from boston massachusetts in 1723.
_ _ _ _ _ _ _ _□_ _ _ _ _ _ _ _ _

5. City Hall, one of the largest city halls in the world, is on broad street.
_ _ _ _□_ _ _□_ _

6. Congress often met in this city during the revolutionary war.
_ _ _ _□_ _ _ _ _ _ _ _ _ _

7. independence hall is one landmark. _ _ _ _□_ _ _ _ _ _ _□_ _ _

8. During the 1700s, this city was the largest and richest city in america.
_ _ _ _ _□_□

The name of this city is _ _ _ _ _ _ _ _ _ _ _ _ .

Macmillan/McGraw-Hill

Mechanics: Abbreviations

An **abbreviation** is a short way to write a word. Begin titles of a person with a **capital letter.** End most titles with a **period.**

    Mrs. Silver   **Dr.** Matthews

Begin abbreviations of days of the week and months of the year with a **capital letter.** End them with a **period.**

    Thursday ⟶ **Thurs.**   February ⟶ **Feb.**
          April ⟶ **Apr.**

A. Circle each correct abbreviation.

1. Ms. Baker	**5.** Mr. Feld	**9.** Aug
2. Mrs Fox	**6.** Nov.	**10.** Dr. Pim
3. Dec.	**7.** Sat	**11.** tues
4. mar.	**8.** Wed.	**12.** Jan.

B. Write whether each underlined abbreviation is a title, a day of the week, or a month of the year.

13. end of Jan.   _____

14. Mr. Rand's dog   _____

15. Dr. Sacks   _____

16. an appointment for Mon.   _____

17. Mrs. Rand   _____

18. Ms. Rand   _____

19. until Wed.   _____

20. by early Feb.   _____

Macmillan/McGraw-Hill

Mechanics: Abbreviations

> An **abbreviation** is the shortened form of a word. Most abbreviations begin with a capital letter and end with a period.
>
> | **titles:** | Dr. Rivera | Mrs. Schwartz |
> |---|---|---|
> | **days:** | Sun. | Thurs. |
> | **months:** | Dec. | Feb. |

A. Write each abbreviation correctly on the first line in each row. On the second line, tell whether the abbreviation is a title, month, or day.

1. jan _____ _____

2. tues _____ _____

3. mr _____ _____

4. Wed. _____ _____

5. dr _____ _____

6. oct. _____ _____

7. Ms _____ _____

8. sat. _____ _____

9. feb _____ _____

10. nov. _____ _____

B. Circle the correct abbreviation for each phrase.

11. a hot day in ____	Aug	Aug.
12. my neighbor ____ Collins	mrs.	Mrs.
13. ____ Weaver	Dr.	Dr
14. by ____	Mon.	mon
15. not until ____	wed.	Wed.

Mechanics: Abbreviations

It's a Date!

Mrs. Brannigan lost her calendar. She can't remember what she has to do and when she has to do it! Work with your group to help Mrs. Brannigan by writing her schedule on the calendar below. Wherever possible, use abbreviations for titles, days, and months.

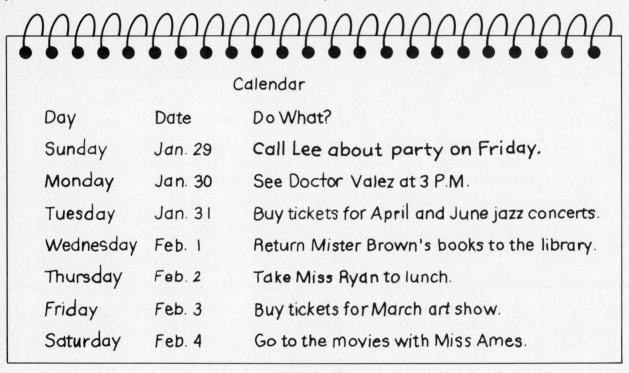

Calendar

Day	Date	Do What?
Sunday	Jan. 29	Call Lee about party on Friday.
Monday	Jan. 30	See Doctor Valez at 3 P.M.
Tuesday	Jan. 31	Buy tickets for April and June jazz concerts.
Wednesday	Feb. 1	Return Mister Brown's books to the library.
Thursday	Feb. 2	Take Miss Ryan to lunch.
Friday	Feb. 3	Buy tickets for March art show.
Saturday	Feb. 4	Go to the movies with Miss Ames.

Calendar

Day	Date	Do What?

Verbs in the Present

> The verbs **am, is,** and **are** tell about the present.
> Each of these verbs must agree with the subject.
>
> **If the subject is**   **use the linking verb**
>
> I ————————————————→ **am**
> a singular noun, **he, she,** or **it** ——→ **is**
> a plural noun, **you, we,** or **they** ——→ **are**
>
> I am a stamp collector.
> Sam is a collector, too.
> We are always busy with our stamp albums.

Read each sentence. Circle the correct verb.

1. Some stamps _____ quite rare.   is   are

2. That stamp _____ very old.   am   is

3. I _____ curious about it.   am   is

4. It _____ very faded.   is   are

5. Rare stamps _____ expensive.   am   are

6. Some stamps _____ worth a fortune.   are   is

7. This one _____ very colorful.   am   is

8. I _____ interested in it.   am   are

9. It _____ not rare.   is   are

10. It _____ not worth much money.   are   is

11. Now Sam _____ here.   am   is

12. I _____ in a hurry.   is   am

13. Sam _____ after a foreign stamp.   is   are

14. We _____ on the collector's trail.   are   is

15. We _____ interested in its price.   am   are

Verbs in the Present

The verbs **am, is,** and **are** tell about the present. Use **am** when the subject is **I.**

I am eight years old.

Use **is** when the subject is **she, he, it,** or a singular noun.

She is a letter carrier.

Use **are** when the subject is **you, we, they,** or a plural noun.

We are on her route.

Rewrite each sentence using the correct form of the verb **be.**

1. My house (is, are) on the mountain.

_____

2. It (is, am) far from town.

_____

3. We (is, are) far from other houses, too.

_____

4. Our mail (is, are) carried on horseback.

_____

5. We (is, are) standing by the mailbox.

_____

6. I (am, are) excited.

_____

7. A special package (is, am) on its way.

_____

8. It (is, are) for me.

_____

Macmillan/McGraw-Hill

Verbs in the Present

Space Station Pen Pal

The following letter to a pen pal was written by a person who lives in a space station. Complete the letter. Some of the missing words are forms of the verb **be.**

Dear Pen Pal,

My name _____ _____ . I _____

_____ years old. My parents _____ scientists who

study _____ . I _____ a _____ .

My space station's name _____ _____ . The

station _____ very _____ . Each day

_____ very _____ here.

You _____ a _____ writer. I _____

_____ that you _____ my _____ .

Your friend,

_____

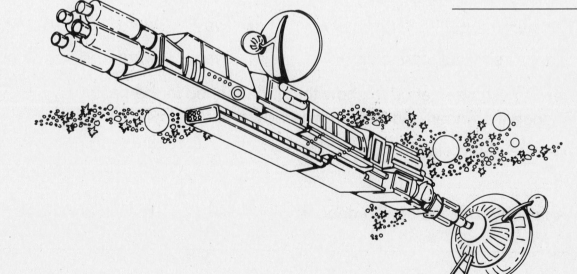

Verbs in the Past

> The verbs **was** and **were** tell about the past.
>
> Each of these verbs must agree with the subject of the sentence.
>
> **If the subject is**   **use the verb**
>
>   a singular noun, **I, it, she,** or **he** ——————→ **was**
>   a plural noun, **we, you,** or **they** ——————→ **were**
>
> The rider <u>was</u> late. ←—— singular subject
> We <u>were</u> very worried. ←—— plural subject

A. Circle the correct verb.

1. The storm ____ bad.   was   were

2. Lightning bolts ____ frequent.   was   were

3. The downpour ____ very heavy.   was   were

4. Roads ____ washed away.   was   were

5. The pony express rider ____ very late.   was   were

6. He ____ a new rider.   was   were

7. His name ____ Link Carpenter.   was   were

8. He ____ sixteen years old.   was   were

B. Rewrite each sentence to show that it happened in the past. Change the underlined verb to **was** or **were.**

9. We <u>are</u> at the station.

_____

10. A tall boy <u>is</u> at the station door.

_____

11. Link <u>is</u> safe with the mail.

_____

Name _____

Verbs in the Past

The verbs **was** and **were** tell about the past.
Use **was** when the subject is **I, she, he, it,** or a singular noun.

   Mail <u>was</u> always late.

Use **were** when the subject is **we, you, they,** or a plural noun.

   People <u>were</u> annoyed.

A. Write **was** or **were** to complete each sentence.

1. In the 1800s, the mail _____ very slow out west.

2. People _____ bothered by long delays.

3. The Pony Express _____ important.

4. It _____ a fast mail delivery service.

5. The route _____ from California to Missouri.

6. The Pony Express _____ a relay system of 190 stations.

7. The stations _____ ten to fifteen miles apart.

8. A fresh horse _____ ready at each station.

B. Rewrite each sentence in the past tense. Use **was** or **were.**

9. Many dangers are along the route.

   _____

10. Pony Express riders are brave.

   _____

11. They are hardworking, too.

   _____

12. A letter is rarely lost.

   _____

Verbs in the Past

The Space Race

You are about to begin a space launch. For each item, draw an arrow from each subject to its correct predicate. Are you ready for countdown? 4 - 3 - 2 - 1 - 0 - BLAST-OFF!

1. Sally Ride   were the first to land on Mars.

American space probes   was the first American woman in space.

2. The Russians   was the first person in space.

Yuri Gargarin   were the first to send an animal into space.

3. *Sputnik I*   was the size of a football.

Two Americans   were the first to walk on the moon.

4. John Glenn, Jr.,   were the first to live in a space station.

Three astronauts   was the first American to orbit the earth.

Mechanics: Contractions

A **contraction** is a shortened form of two words.
In a contraction, one or more letters are left out.

Use an (') to take the place of the missing letter or letters.

is not ⟶ isn't   did not ⟶ didn't
are not ⟶ aren't   do not ⟶ don't
have not ⟶ haven't   should not ⟶ shouldn't
cannot ⟶ can't   was not ⟶ wasn't

The word **won't** is a special contraction. In this contraction, the spelling of **will** changes.

will not ⟶ won't

A. Underline the contraction in each sentence. Circle the two words that make up the contraction.

1. This letter isn't for me.   is not   had not

2. I can't read the name.   could not   cannot

3. The letters aren't clear.   are not   is not

4. I don't know the writer.   did not   do not

5. I shouldn't throw the letter out.   should not   are not

6. It wasn't meant for me.   was not   were not

7. It couldn't be for Mama.   could not   can not

8. We haven't asked Dad if it is his.   has not   have not

B. Look at the first two words in each row. Then circle the contraction formed from these words.

9. **had not**   haven't   hadn't   hasn't

10. **was not**   wasn't   wouldn't   won't

11. **will not**   wasn't   won't   wouldn't

12. **could not**   aren't   can't   couldn't

Mechanics: Contractions

A **contraction** is a shortened form of two words. One or more letters are left out.

An **apostrophe (')** takes the place of the missing letter or letters.

did + not = didn't   can + not = can't   have + not = haven't

The word **won't** is a special contraction. The spelling of **will** changes.

will + not = won't

A. Circle the contraction in each sentence. Write the two words that form the contraction.

1. Once, there weren't any post offices.   _____   _____

2. People didn't send letters the way we do now.   _____   _____

3. Runners carried letters, but they wouldn't go too far.   _____   _____

4. Some people couldn't write words.   _____   _____

5. When people didn't write words, they made pictures.   _____   _____

B. Combine each word from the box with the word **not** to form a contraction. Write the contractions on the lines.

should	will
has	are
is	do

_____   _____

_____   _____

_____   _____

Mechanics: Contractions

Contractions Across and Down

Work with your partner to circle the two words in each sentence that can be made into a contraction. Write the contraction on the line. Put each letter or apostrophe on a separate space. Then write the word that completes the sentence at the bottom of the page. To do this, write the circled letters in order, from top to bottom.

1. The show would not start on time.

___ ___ ___ ___ ___ ___ ___ ___

2. Jody can not find her costume. _Ⓞ_ ___ ___ ___ ___

3. The magician's rabbit will not go in the hat. ___ Ⓞ ___ ___ ___

4. The audience should not be seated.

___ ___ ___ ___ ___ Ⓞ ___ ___

5. Audiences do not like to wait. ___ ___ ___ ___ Ⓞ

6. The tap dancers were not ready.

___ ___ Ⓞ ___ ___ ___ ___

7. The acrobats are not even there. _Ⓞ_ ___ ___ ___ ___

8. A singer could not find her music.

Ⓞ ___ ___ ___ ___ ___ ___

9. The scenery did not stay up. ___ ___ ___ ___ ___ Ⓞ

10. The popcorn is not popping. _Ⓞ_ ___ ___ ___ ___

11. One actor does not want to go on.

___ Ⓞ ___ ___ ___ ___

12. The tickets have not been sold. ___ ___ ___ ___ Ⓞ ___ ___

13. The show was not well planned. ___ ___ Ⓞ ___ ___ ___

14. The children had not thought ahead. ___ ___ ___ ___ ___ ___

You haven't any trouble making _____

Name _____

What Is Special About the Verb *be*?

Action verbs ⟶ tell about actions.

Action verbs tell what someone or something does or did.

   Lina and I <u>play</u> together.

The special verb **be** does not tell about actions.

The special verb **be** tells what someone or something is or is like.

The words **am, is, are, was,** and **were** are all forms of the verb **be.**

   Lina <u>is</u> my cousin.   We <u>are</u> close.

A. Read each sentence. If there is an action verb, circle it. If there is a form of the verb **be,** underline it.

1. My family is Hispanic.

2. Some of us are from Puerto Rico.

3. Others live in Spain.

4. We are a close family.

5. We write to each other.

6. We visit each other, too.

7. Lina is my favorite cousin.

8. She is nine years old.

9. I am a bit younger.

10. We like each other very much.

B. On the lines below, copy each sentence that has a form of the verb **be.**

11. Lina and I are alike.
12. She is a good reader.
13. I read a lot, too.
14. We share books long distance.
15. We are great friends.

_____

_____

_____

_____

What Is Special About the Verb *be*?

> Some verbs are special forms of the verb **be.** They do not name actions.
>
> **Am, is, are, was,** and **were** are all forms of the verb **be.**
>
> The special verb **be** tells what someone or something is or is like.
>
> I am Danny. Kevin is my friend.
>
> These verbs must agree with the subject of the sentence.
>
> This letter is for me. The letters are for me.

A. Read each sentence. If there is an action verb, circle it. If there is a form of the verb **be,** underline it.

1. This letter is from Kevin.

2. He lives in Quebec City, Canada.

3. Kevin was just eight.

4. He goes to a small school in Quebec.

5. He walks a mile to school each day.

6. Quebec City is very old.

7. Some buildings are ancient.

B. Some of the sentences below have action verbs. Others have a form of the verb **be.** Draw one line under the action verb. Draw two lines under the form of the verb **be.** Circle the subject that each verb agrees with.

8. We visit Kevin's family.

9. They are delighted to meet us.

10. I am thrilled to meet them.

11. Kevin speaks both French and English.

12. Now we write twice a month.

Macmillan/McGraw-Hill

What Is Special About the Verb *be*?

Mystery Country

Put a ✓ in the box next to each sentence that has a form of the verb **be.** Circle this verb. Then, on the lines, write the underlined letter in each checked sentence to spell the name of a country.

[ ] **1.** John C̲abot was one of the men who explored here. _____

[ ] **2.** T̲he sun shines 24 hours a day in the summer. _____

[ ] **3.** Ottawa is the capital of this country. _____

[ ] **4.** People c̲elebrate Independence Day in September. _____

[ ] **5.** The Spanish ruled this country for 300 y̲ears. _____

[ ] **6.** Montreal and Toront̲o are the two largest cities. _____

[ ] **7.** French and English a̲re its official languages. _____

[ ] **8.** Commodore Perry s̲ailed there in 1853. _____

[ ] **9.** Llamas live ther̲e. _____

[ ] **10.** Farmers grow bananas t̲here. _____

[ ] **11.** It is the second l̲argest country in the world. _____

[ ] **12.** People build dikes t̲here. _____

[ ] **13.** Christopher Columbus l̲anded there in 1492. _____

[ ] **14.** Some settlers who came there we̲re from France. _____

The name of the mystery country is _____.

Grammar and Writing Connection:
Using *I* and *me*

Use **I** and **me** when you talk or write about yourself.

If you talk about yourself and another person, always put yourself last.

Shari and I write a lot.

Beth writes to Shari and me.

If you want to figure out whether to use **I** or **me,** leave out the other noun.

Beth sent ~~Jake and~~ me a book.

~~Jake and~~ I read the book immediately.

Circle the pronoun in ( ) that completes each sentence.

1. (I, Me) often write to Shari.
2. She writes back to (I, me) quickly.
3. Mom and (I, me) decide to call Shari.
4. Mom gives (I, me) the telephone number.
5. (I, Me) dial the long distance operator.
6. Soon (I, me) hear Shari on the line.
7. "Hello," (I, me) yell over the wire.
8. Shari speaks to Mom and (I, me) for a while.
9. She and (I, me) have a lot to say.
10. Shari invites (I, me) for a visit.
11. (I, Me) turn to Mom.
12. Mom gives (I, me) permission to go.

Name
_____

Subject Pronouns

> A **subject pronoun** is a word that replaces one or more nouns in the subject part of a sentence.
>
> Jill and I leave for Thrill Park.
>
> We leave early in the morning.

A. Write the pronoun and verb in each sentence.

1. We get to the amusement park. _____

2. It is brand new. _____

3. I go on the giant slide. _____

4. He collects the ticket. _____

5. You ride the merry-go-round. _____

6. They climb on the horses. _____

7. She reaches for the gold ring. _____

8. We run to the fun house. _____

B. Circle the verb that correctly completes each sentence.

9. I (find, finds) the roller coaster.

10. We (wait, waits) on line.

11. It (is, are) our turn.

12. She (take, takes) a seat.

13. I (sit, sits) beside Meg.

14. They (fasten, fastens) their safety belts.

15. He (start, starts) the engine.

16. You (hold, holds) on tightly.

17. It (fly, flies) around the tracks.

Macmillan/McGraw-Hill

Grammar and Writing Connection:
Using *I* and *me*

Guess Who

A. Write **I** or **me** to complete the riddle clues. Then circle the answer to the riddle.

1. George Washington and _____ both had the same job.

They celebrate holidays for George and _____ .

George and _____ have our pictures on stamps.

You can find _____ on pennies, too.

Who am I?   Ben Franklin   Thomas Jefferson   Abraham Lincoln

2. Sojourner Truth and _____ were both born as slaves.

People called _____ *Moses* .

Sojourner and _____ helped free slaves.

Slave owners wanted to capture _____ .

Who am I?   Betsy Ross   Florence Nightingale   Harriet Tubman

3. My brother and _____ made the first plane.

He helped _____ to test the plane.

_____ flew the plane for the first time, while by brother watched.

Who am I?   Amelia Earhart   Orville Wright   John Glenn

B. Write your own riddle for a famous person. The person can be living or dead. Use **I** and **me** in your clues. Share your riddle with a partner.

_____

_____

_____

_____

_____

What Is a Pronoun?

A **pronoun** takes the place of one or more nouns.

Annie takes a shot.   Max and Dean stand up.
She scores.   They cheer for Annie.

A **singular pronoun** names one person, place, or thing,

singular pronouns ———→ **I, you, he, she, it,
me, you, him, her, it**

A **plural pronoun** names more than one person, place, or thing.

plural pronouns ———→ **we, they, you,
us, you, them**

A. Read each sentence. Circle the word that tells if the underlined pronoun is singular or plural.

1. She holds the ball.   singular   plural

2. Mark dribbles it.   singular   plural

3. Ken and Amy watch him.   singular   plural

4. They want the Jets to win.   singular   plural

5. I toss the ball.   singular   plural

6. The player catches it.   singular   plural

7. He takes a shot.   singular   plural

8. You can see the ball go in.   singular   plural

9. The shot scores more points for them.   singular   plural

10. We take a break.   singular   plural

B. Circle the pronoun or pronouns in each sentence.

11. Did you hear it?   14. He takes two foul shots.

12. They blew the whistle.   15. He misses both of them.

13. We start again.   16. I grab the ball!

What Is a Pronoun?

A **pronoun** is a word that takes the place of one or more nouns.

Amy raises her hand.   Pat and Cindy look at their books.
She asks a question.   They answer the question.

A **singular pronoun** names one person, place, or thing.

singular pronouns ⟶ **I, you, he, she, it
me, you, him, her, it**

A **plural pronoun** names more than one person, place, or thing.

plural pronouns ⟶ **we, they, you, us, you, them**

A. Read each sentence. Write **singular** or **plural** to tell what each underlined pronoun is.

1. We arrive at the courts.   _____

2. The player waves to me.   _____

3. He is a fine player.   _____

4. I watch from the stands.   _____

5. People cheer them on.   _____

6. It is a very close game.   _____

7. They both serve well.   _____

8. Tell us the score.   _____

9. Let her play the winner.   _____

B. Circle the correct verb to complete each sentence.

10. She _____ a new racket.   (has, have)

11. It _____ stronger than the other one. (is, are)

12. She _____ Roberto to try it.   (allow, allows)

13. They _____ back and forth.   (volley, volleys)

14. We _____ the score.   (announce, announces)

What Is a Pronoun?

Double-Crosser

Cross out one letter in each square going across or down to find the hidden pronoun. Write that pronoun in the sentence clue with the same number. Remember to begin the first word in a sentence with a capital letter.

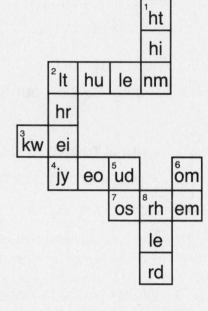

| him | you | us | her | me | them | they | she | we |

ACROSS

2. Jean likes muffins.

She likes to bake _____ .

3. My brother and I like spaghetti.

_____ eat it with meatballs.

4. I like mushrooms.

Do _____ like mushrooms?

7. Arlene likes carrot sticks.

_____ eats them with dip.

DOWN

1. Jo cooks with Grandpa.

She likes to cook with _____ .

2. Jo and Grandpa bake bread.

_____ put bananas in it.

5. My mom calls my brother and me.

Mom made eggs for _____ .

6. Mom also made some waffles.

She gave _____ three.

8. My brother thanked Mom.

He gave _____ a big hug.

Singular Possessive Nouns

> A **possessive noun** shows ownership. It tells what someone or something owns or has.
>
> To form a singular possessive noun, add **'s** to the singular noun.
>
> **singular noun + 's** = singular possessive noun
>
> man   + 's = man's
>
> dog   + 's = dog's
>
>   the **boy's** photo   the **man's** painting

A. Write the possessive noun in each sentence.

1. Jill's painting is colorful.   _____

2. Tom's picture is huge.   _____

3. The teacher's book is lost.   _____

4. Maria's painting is in the art show, too.   _____

5. The judge's name is Robert Baron.   _____

6. That big sculpture is Kevin's.   _____

7. I want to see that girl's photo again.   _____

8. Anne's picture won the blue ribbon.   _____

9. I thought Dan's painting was better.   _____

B. Choose a possessive noun from the box. Write it on the correct line.

> dog's   winner's   artist's   bird's

---

10. the _____ painting

11. the _____ nest

12. the _____ bone

13. the _____ prize

Singular Possessive Nouns

A **possessive noun** shows ownership. It tells what someone or something owns or has. Add an apostrophe and an **s** (**'s**) to the singular noun.

Penny**'s** sneakers   the boy**'s** bicycle

A. Circle the possessive noun in each sentence.

1. The team's colors are gold and red.

2. Ted's jacket is lost.

3. Where is Fran's helmet?

4. What is the team captain's name?

5. Rusty's brother is on the team.

6. The newest bike is Brian's.

7. Adam's bike is the fastest.

8. Meg's bike has new tires.

9. That girl's bike has red reflectors.

10. Ken's bike needs new brakes.

B. Write the possessive form of each singular noun.

11. Jan _____

12. lion _____

13. Dr. Ryan _____

14. Mom _____

15. friend _____

16. coach _____

17. Ms. Cohen _____

18. country _____

19. writer _____

20. Mr. Reed _____

21. man _____

22. dog _____

23. Lynne _____

24. brother _____

Macmillan/McGraw-Hill

Possessive Nouns

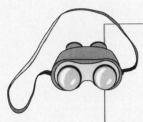

Focus on Possessive Nouns

- A **possessive noun** shows that someone or something owns or has something.
- Add an apostrophe and an **s** ('s) to a singular noun to make it possessive.
- Add an apostrophe (') to make most plural nouns possessive.
- Add an apostrophe and an **s** ('s) to plural nouns that don't end in **s** to make them possessive.

Who has what? Underline the incorrect possessive nouns in these sentences. Write the correct form in the blank.

- The rabbits tail was soft and white. _____

- The two sisters hats blew off in the wind. _____

- The mans boss left that umbrella here. _____

- When the mouses cage gets dirty, we have to clean it out. _____

- At the library, the childrens room is cozy and filled with

  neat books. _____

Fun Favorites

Do your friends or family have toys or games you like? For each toy or game you can think of, write one or two sentences. Tell to whom it belongs and why you like it. Check your possessive nouns.

Mechanics: Contractions

Contractions
- are a shortened form of two words.
- are two words joined together to make one word.
- leave out one or more letters.

Use an apostrophe (') to replace the letter or letters that are left out.

Here are some contractions:

I + am = I'm	he + will = he'll
he + is = he's	we + will = we'll
she + is = she's	they + will = they'll
it + is = it's	I + will = I'll
you + are = you're	it + will = it'll
they + are = they're	you + have = you've
we + are = we're	we + have = we've
she + will = she'll	they + have = they've
you + will = you'll	I + have = I've

A. Circle the contraction in each sentence.

1. I'm going on a trip.
2. What a wonderful trip it'll be!
3. We're going by car.
4. We'll be gone for a week.
5. She'll bring her camera along.
6. He's doing most of the driving.
7. They'll meet us in Canada.
8. We've been there before.
9. It's a beautiful country.
10. I've always loved it there.

B. Circle the two words that each underlined contraction stands for.

11.	they'll	they will	they can	she will
12.	he's	he will	he is	it is
13.	we've	they have	we are	we have
14.	you're	you will	you are	we are
15.	I'm	I will	I am	it is

Mechanics: Contractions

Contractathon!

Draw lines from each word on the left to each possible correct contraction ending on the right. Find as many contractions as you can.

I		'll
we		's
they		're
she		'm
you		've
it		

Use some of the contractions above to finish the riddles. Remember to begin the first word in a sentence with a capital letter.

1. Why is the letter <u>a</u> like <u>noon</u>?

_____ in the middle of <u>day</u>.

2. There are ten cats in a boat. One jumps out. How many are left?

None. _____ all copycats.

3. What did one elevator say to the other elevator?

"I think _____ coming down with something."

Macmillan/McGraw-Hill

Contractions

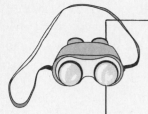

Focus on Contractions

- A **contraction** is a shortened form of two words.
- An **apostrophe** (') shows where one or more letters have been left out.

Leave out some letters in the words below to form contractions. After each sentence, write the contraction in the blank.

- Kay, you have not seen the new pet shop? _____

- My brother has not felt well all week. _____

- Today I am feeling better. _____

- Hakim, would not you like to go for a walk? _____

- No thanks, I do not care for lima beans. _____

Say P-l-e-a-s-e

Your teacher has asked you to write a story called "Good Manners" for the school newspaper. Choose two or three topics to write about. Don't forget to use contractions correctly.

Macmillan/McGraw-Hill

Adjectives That Compare

> To compare two nouns ————————→ use **adjective** + **er**
>   My dog Pip is **smaller** than my cat.
>
> To compare more than two nouns ——→ use **adjective** + **est**
>   He is the **smallest** pet in our home.

A. Underline the correct adjective in ( ) to complete each sentence.

1. Pip's legs are (shorter, shortest) than my cat's legs.
2. Pip's legs are the (shorter, shortest) I've ever seen.
3. Pip's ears are the (long, longest) of any dog's.
4. But Pip is (faster, fastest) than my cat.
5. His legs are (strong, stronger) than most.
6. Pip's fur is (longer, longest) than my cat's fur.
7. His fur is the (longer, longest) of any dog in our neighborhood.
8. My cat is (meaner, meanest) than Pip.
9. My cat is the (meaner, meanest) animal we own.

B. Write each sentence. Use the correct form of the adjective in ( ).

10. Pip's eyes are (bright) than my cat's eyes.

_____

_____

11. Pip is the (young) animal we own.

_____

_____

12. Pip is the (kind) dog in our neighborhood.

_____

_____

Adjectives That Compare

> To compare two nouns, add **er** to the adjective.
>   Betty is <u>faster</u> than Billy.
>
> To compare more than two nouns, add **est** to the adjective.
>   Betty is the <u>fastest</u> dolphin in the aquarium.

A. Circle the correct adjective for each sentence.

1. Dolphins are (smart, smarter) than sharks.

2. Dolphins are among the (smarter, smartest) animals in the world.

3. Dolphins are (smaller, smallest) than whales.

4. They are (kinder, kindest) than other animals.

5. Some dolphins are the (higher, highest) jumpers in the sea.

B. Write each sentence using the correct form of the adjective in (   ).

6. Billy is the (old) dolphin in the aquarium.

_____

7. Barney makes (high) jumps than Betty.

_____

8. Billy moves the (slow) of the three.

_____

9. Betty seems (strong) than Billy.

_____

10. She is the (long) dolphin of all.

_____

Adjectives That Compare

Comparatively Speaking

A. Pretend that you discovered a new animal in the jungle. It is called a jatterwack. Complete the sentences that compare the jatterwack to other animals. Choose adjectives from the box. Write their correct forms on the lines.

sharp	wild	grand	quick
tall	shy	loud	short
kind	round	smooth	rough

1. It is _____ than a seal.

2. It is _____ than a giraffe.

3. Its claws are _____ than a crab's.

4. Its growl is _____ than a lion's.

5. It is the _____ animal I know.

B. Now draw a picture of the jatterwack in the space below.

Using *a*, *an*, and *the*

The words **a, an,** and **the** are special adjectives.
They are called articles.

The articles **a** and **an** are used before singular nouns.

a parrot   an eagle

If the noun begins with a consonant sound, use **a.**

a lion   a tiger

If the noun begins with a vowel, use **an.**

an elephant   an antelope

The article **the** is used before singular or plural nouns.

the seal   the animals

Circle the correct article in ( ) to complete each sentence.

1. Janet Doran is (a, an) zoo keeper.

2. She loves all (the, an) animals in the zoo.

3. To her, each animal is (a, an) pet.

4. There is (a, an) new baby tiger.

5. Janet feeds (the, an) baby with a bottle.

6. The baby tiger is (a, an) delight.

7. It cuddles up to Janet like (a, an) kitten.

8. There is (a, an) old elephant at the zoo, too.

9. Janet has known (a, the) elephant for a long time.

10. She gives the animal (a, an) bag of peanuts each day.

11. (A, The) elephant waits for Janet to come.

12. It treats Janet like (a, an) friend.

13. Janet's favorite animal is (the, an) walrus.

Macmillan/McGraw-Hill

Using *a*, *an*, and *the*

> Use **a** before singular nouns that begin with a consonant.
> Use **an** before singular nouns that begin with a vowel.
>
>   <u>a</u> snake   <u>an</u> insect
>
> Use **the** before singular and plural nouns.
>
>   <u>The</u> snake is sleeping on the rocks.

A. Complete each sentence with the correct article in the (   ).

1. The snake is _____ kind of reptile.   (a, an)

2. On land, _____ snake slides around on its belly.   (an, the)

3. A snake often coils into _____ ball.   (a, an)

4. I found _____ snake in my backyard.   (a, an)

5. It hungrily ate _____ earthworm.   (a, an)

6. Luckily, _____ reptile was harmless.   (an, the)

7. I kept the creature for _____ pet.   (a, an)

B. Write **a, an,** or **the** in each blank.

8. I made _____ terrarium for _____ snake.

9. I gave it _____ name Mike.

10. It was a young garter snake, not _____ adult.

11. I found _____ bowl and some rocks.

12. I put them into _____ terrarium.

13. I filled _____ tub with water.

14. Mike took a swim and sat on _____ rocks.

15. I feel like _____ expert on garter snakes.

Using *a*, *an*, and *the*

The Riddler

Complete each riddle question and answer. Write two different articles.
Use **a** and **an** or **a** and **the**.

1. What time is it when _____ elephant sits on your fence?

   It's time to get _____ fence that is new.

2. How can you tell which end of _____ worm is its head?

   Tickle it in _____ middle and see which end smiles.

3. What is _____ spider that has written books called?

   It is called _____ author.

4. How do you make _____ egg roll?

   Push it down _____ hill.

5. What will happen to _____ people who tickle a mule?

   They will get _____ kick out of it.

6. Why does _____ hummingbird hum?

   It hums because it doesn't know _____ words.

7. When is _____ cook mean?

   He is mean when he beats _____ eggs.

8. Where do _____ butchers dance?

   They dance at _____ meatball.

Macmillan/McGraw-Hill

Grammar and Writing Connection:
Using Contractions Correctly

The word **not** is a negative word.

Words that have *no* in them are also called **negative words.** Here are some examples.

no	none	nothing
nobody	no one	nowhere

Do not use two negative words in one sentence.

I <u>didn't</u> get any mail this week. ⟶ correct

I <u>didn't</u> get <u>no</u> mail this week. ⟶ not correct

A. Circle the negative words in each pair of sentences. Then underline the sentence that is correct.

1. Sal didn't get no packages delivered.

Sal didn't get any packages delivered.

2. I haven't got any stamps.

I haven't got no stamps.

3. I won't send no letters today.

I won't send any letters today.

4. He didn't send me nothing.

He didn't send me anything.

B. Rewrite each sentence. Use only one negative word.

6. We didn't buy no stamps.

_____

6. Ken hasn't received no letters.

_____

7. They haven't gotten nothing in the mail.

_____

Grammar and Writing Connection:
Using Contractions Correctly

Two **negative words** cannot be used in the same sentence.
If a sentence has a contraction that is formed with the word **not,** no other negative word can be used.
Here are some examples of negative words:

no	none	nothing
nobody	no one	no where

Correct: I didn't mail any packages today.
Not correct: I didn't mail no packages today.

Rewrite the letter. Write each sentence so that there is only one negative word.

Dear Max,

   I didn't have no time to write before. This new dog of mine isn't no fun. He doesn't do nothing. He doesn't perform no tricks. He doesn't eat no dog food. He won't listen to nothing I say. I didn't have no idea what owning a dog would be like. Next time I won't get no pet. I'll buy a computer, instead.

                               Your friend,
                               Greg

_____

_____

_____

_____

_____

_____

_____

_____

Double Negatives

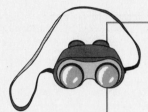

Focus on Double Negatives

- A **negative** is a word that means **no**. Never use two negatives in one sentence when telling about the same person or thing.
- Common negatives: **no, can't, never, not, don't, nothing**

Can you use negatives correctly? Don't say no! Choose the correct word in parentheses. Write the word in the blank.

- Don't you have (anything, nothing) to write

  with? _____

- There can't be (any, no) pets in the restaurant.

  _____

- Manuel and Isabel didn't catch (no, any) fish yet.

  _____

- Luciana doesn't (ever, never) eat beets.

  _____

Shhh! HOSPITAL

You are the director of a children's hospital. Write a poster that tells visitors about the rules they must follow when they come to see children in your hospital. Draw a picture under the rules. Don't use any double negatives.

Mechanics: Commas
in a Series

A list of three or more words is called a series.

Use **commas** (,) to separate the words in a series.
Remember to use a comma **before** the word **and.**

The circus is fun , thrilling , and unforgettable.

The animals are big , medium-sized , and small.

A. Underline the sentence in each pair that is correctly punctuated.

1. Lola Nesbit trains lions, bears, and elephants.
Lola Nesbit trains lions bears and elephants.

2. The lions seem strong mean and scary.
The lions seem strong, mean, and scary.

3. But they are really quiet, gentle, and well-trained.
But they are really quiet gentle and well-trained.

B. In each sentence, underline the words in the series.
Rewrite the sentence using commas where they belong.

4. There is a mother father and baby bear.

_____

_____

5. The bears ride bicycles dance and juggle.

_____

_____

6. They are smart funny and quite playful.

_____

_____

Macmillan/McGraw-Hill

Name _____

Mechanics: Commas in a Series

A **series** is a list of three or more words.
Always use **commas** to separate the words in a series.

The pet shop was light, big, and colorful.

There were animals, pet supplies, and cages everywhere.

Rewrite each sentence using commas where they belong.

1. Bird cages held parrots canaries and parakeets.

_____

_____

2. The feathered animals were noisy colorful and active.

_____

_____

3. Dogs rabbits and hamsters won the customers' hearts.

_____

_____

4. They were small furry and cute.

_____

_____

5. Fish snakes and lizards were also for sale.

_____

_____

6. The fish were tiny colorful and inexpensive to buy.

_____

_____

Mechanics: Commas in a Series

This, That, and the Other

Each picture goes with the sentence next to it. Rewrite the underlined part of each sentence. Add commas where they belong.

A good night's sleep makes you healthy wealthy and wise.

1. _____

_____

Rain snow and sleet do not stop the mail.

2. _____

_____

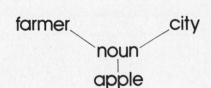

farmer ____ city
noun
apple

A noun is a word that names a person place or thing.

3. _____

_____

A doctor can check your eyes ears and nose .

4. _____

_____

Our favorite flavors are vanilla chocolate and strawberry.

5. _____

_____

Capitalization and Punctuation of Quotations

Use **quotation marks** to show that somebody is speaking. Quotation marks come at the beginning and end of a person's exact words.
   Sono asked, "Do you like to dance?"

Capitalize the first word of a direct quotation.
   Andrew added, "**D**ancing is great exercise."

Place a period inside closing quotation marks.
   The teacher said, "The recital will be in two weeks**.**"

Place a **question mark** or an **exclamation point** inside the quotation marks when it is part of the quotation.
   "Is that enough time to practice**?**" Mary inquired.

Rewrite the sentences correctly on the lines below.

1. "what should we do after school? Diego asked.

_____

2. I replied, do you want to watch television at my house?

_____

3. "That is too boring! shouted Diego.

_____

4. do you have any better ideas"? I challenged.

_____

5. He suggested, Yes, we can visit the dinosaur exhibit at the museum".

_____

Capitalization and Punctuation of Quotations

Quotation marks come at the beginning and end of a person's exact words. **Capitalize** the first word of a quotation.

Place a **period** inside closing quotation marks.
Place a **question mark** or an **exclamation point** inside the quotation marks when it is part of the quotation.

"Let's play a trick on Susan!" they all cried.

Rewrite the following sentences using the correct capitalization and punctuation.

1. He said, the movie is showing in town.

_____

2. Frank remarked, the hiking trail is ten miles long.

_____

3. "what a beautiful view! Yvette cried.

_____

4. do you want to go fishing today? my brother asked.

_____

5. what is so funny? Kevin asked

_____

6. this milk is sour! Anthony complained.

_____

Macmillan/McGraw-Hill

Capitalization and Punctuation of Quotations

You Can Quote Me on That

A. Complete each sentence with a quotation from the speech bubbles above. Correct the capitalization and punctuation of each sentence.

1. _____

_____ asked Melvin.

2. Mitsuko said, _____

_____

3. Janet added, _____

_____

4. _____

_____ asked Jorge.

5. _____

exclaimed Cathy.

B. Rewrite the following sentences correctly.

6. Sekou said, There is more to Ghanaian music than drumming"

_____

7. He continued, "one popular style today is called highlife.

_____

Name _____

Capitalization and Punctuation of Quotations

Use **quotation marks** to show that somebody is speaking. **Quotation marks** come at the beginning and end of a person's exact words.

Capitalize the first word of a direct quotation.
Place a **period** inside closing quotation marks.
Place a **question mark** or an **exclamation point** inside the quotation marks when it is part of the quotation.
Use a **comma** to separate a phrase, such as *he said*, from the quotation itself.

"**B**aseball is fun**,**" he said.

When the speaker's name comes first in the sentence, use a **comma** before the quotation. When the speaker's name follows the quotation, use a **period** after the name.

Marco said, "I love tacos!"
"I love tacos!" said Marco.

A. Circle the errors in each sentence of the conversation below.

Mrs. Kiniry announced, "t his year I'm planning a talent show."

"Can anyone enter"? Kelly asked

"If you have talent, you can enter," Mrs. Kiniry said

 I'll sing!   Kelly cried.

 I can play the piano !" Hector shouted.

Mrs. Kiniry suggested "Maybe you can do an act together.

"that's a great idea!" They agreed.

Capitalization and Punctuation of Quotations

Use **quotation marks** to show that somebody is speaking. Quotation marks come at the beginning and end of a person's exact words.

Capitalize the first word of a direct quotation. Place a period inside closing quotation marks. Place a question mark or an exclamation mark inside the quotation marks when it is part of the quotation.

"Turn down the television!" Mom cried.
"Do you recycle?" my neighbor asked.
"I'm trying out for the lead role," Stephen bragged.

Use a comma to separate a phrase, such as *he said,* from the quotation itself.

"When dinner ends, I will wash the dishes," he said.

When the speaker's name comes first in the sentence, use a **comma** before the quotation. When the speaker's name follows the quotation, use a **period** after the name.

Circle the errors in the following conversation. Then rewrite it correctly on another sheet of paper.

Mom said I could have a pet," Gerard said
_____

What kind of pet do you want?" asked Jen.
_____

Gerard replied. "I'm not sure"
_____

"How about a monkey?   suggested Jen.
_____

Gerard said   I think it would be too hard to take care of.
_____

Jen said   The animal shelter has a lot of pets who need good homes.
_____

Would you go there with me?" Gerard asked.
_____

Sure. Maybe I'll get a pet, too"! Jen replied.
_____

Capitalization and Punctuation of Quotations

Out-of-This-World Quotations

Bollywood Studios has dreamed up an exciting science fiction adventure movie. They have a great cast, a great crew, and a great story. Now they need some great dialog. The paragraphs below tell part of the story. Fill in the blanks with quotations you think would sound good on the big screen. Be sure to use correct capitalization and punctuation.

The Mingus Mission

Max Khan and Nuria Valdes step out of their spaceship and onto Planet

Mingus. Nuria says to Max, _____

He asks, _____

Suddenly they sense that they are no longer alone. A strange voice warns

them, _____

Max exclaims, _____

_____ says Nuria as she leaps

into action. The voice shouts back, _____

_____

One hour later, things are calm. _____

Nuria replies, _____

They reboard their ship to get something to eat. Nuria sighs and says, _____

_____

The Mingus Mission has just begun.

Macmillan/McGraw-Hill

Capitalization and Punctuation of Titles of Works

Capitalize the first word and all important words in the titles of books, short stories, songs, and poems.

<u>The Lion, the Witch, and the Wardrobe</u>

Use **italics** or **underlining** to set off the title of a book.
Use **quotation marks** around the title of a short story, a song, or a poem.

Book: <u>My Life in the Third Grade</u>
Short Story: "Little Red Riding Hood"
Song: "America, the Beautiful"
Poem: "Who Am I?"

A. Use correct capitalization and punctuation to write the following titles.

1. Book: the incredible journey

_____

2. Poem: my woolen sweater itches me

_____

3. Song: The star spangled banner"

_____

4. Short Story: stone soup

_____

B. Write your favorite book, poem, song, film, and short story on the lines.

5. My favorite book _____

6. My favorite song _____

7. My favorite film _____

Capitalization and Punctuation of Titles of Works

Use **quotation marks** around the title of a short story.
 "Jack and the Beanstalk"

Use **quotation marks** around the title of a poem.
 "The Toad"

Use **quotation marks** around the title of a song.
 "Go Tell It on the Mountain"

Use **italics** or **underlining** to set off the title of a book.
 Cloudy with a Chance of Meatballs

Capitalize the first word and each important word. Short words—for example, *and, of,* and *the*—are not capitalized.

Rewrite the following titles using correct capitalization and punctuation.

1. autumn leaves (poem)

_____

2. ben franklin's glass armonica (book)

_____

3. charlotte's web (book)

_____

4. the telephone call (poem)

_____

5. a week in the life of best friends (poem)

_____

6. what a wonderful world (song)

_____

Capitalizing and Punctuating Titles of Works

A. Rewrite each sentence correctly on the line provided.

1. Did you enjoy the poem In Memory"?

_____

2. I'm writing a humorous novel called For the love of cheese.

_____

3. Spider Ananse is a character in Ashley Bryan's story The dancing granny."

_____

4. Gail's favorite book is "Ramona the Brave" by Beverly Cleary.

_____

5. We listened to the song "jump" by Kris Kross.

_____

B. The descriptions below tell about imaginary works. Read each description, and then suggest a title using correct capitalization and punctuation.

6. a short story about a girl's first day of school in a new town

_____

7. a follow-up book to <u>50 Simple Things Kids Can Do to Save the Earth</u> that describes not-so-simple ways that children can help protect the planet

_____

8. a ten-line poem celebrating the beauties of winter

_____

9. a mystery novel about a strange house with secret rooms

_____

Vocabulary Building:
Homophones

Homophones

- are words that sound the same.
- have different spellings.
- have different meanings.

by–buy

hole–whole

I walk by his house.
I buy some apples.

pail–pale

The baby dug a hole.
He ate the whole apple.

The water is in the pail.
I like pale colors.

Circle the pair of words in each box that are homophones.

1. ate eight came same even ever	**5.** help head he'll heel read dear	**9.** climb time best better beet beat
2. pie tie aunt ant blue black	**6.** brake break brush broom fake lake	**10.** sing song I eye rope mope
3. float goat fare fair pace pack	**7.** flip slip sell set blew blue	**11.** berry bury line pine ball back
4. very vase these those choose chews	**8.** man men pen plane main mane	**12.** cent sent boat boot beast barn

Macmillan/McGraw-Hill

Vocabulary Building:
Homophones

Homophones are words that sound the same, but have different spellings and different meanings.

Will you be there?
A bee can sting.

A. Read the word in the first column. Find a word in the sentence that sounds the same as this word. Write that word on the line.

1. **by**   We buy food for the picnic.   _____

2. **too**   Dan picks out two melons.   _____

3. **way**   We weigh them on the scale.   _____

4. **flower** I get some flour for baking.   _____

5. **bred**   I want to make some bread.   _____

6. **there**   The boys will bring their salads.   _____

7. **wood**   Fried chicken would be nice, too.   _____

B. Write a sentence for each pair of homophones. The first one is done for you.

8. pail, pale
   The pale girl filled her pail with shells. _____

9. right, write

   _____

10. won, one

   _____

11. deer, dear

   _____

12. ate, eight

   _____

Vocabulary Building:
Homophones

At the Movies

Work with your group to write a pair of homophones from the box to complete each sentence. You will not use all of the words.

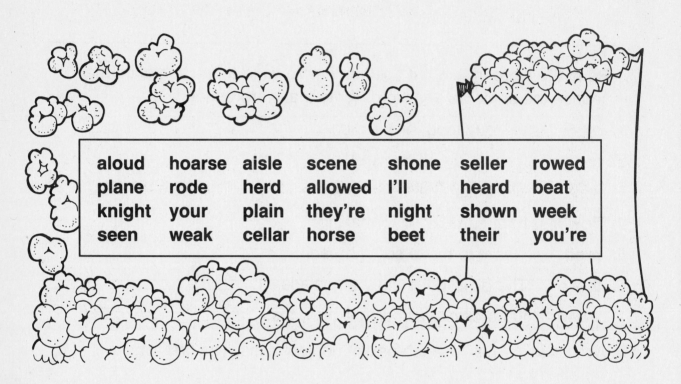

aloud	hoarse	aisle	scene	shone	seller	rowed
plane	rode	herd	allowed	I'll	heard	beat
knight	your	plain	they're	night	shown	week
seen	weak	cellar	horse	beet	their	you're

1. Kate, _____ not in _____ seat.

2. Mike, _____ be sitting in the _____ seat.

3. You aren't _____ to speak _____ in the theater.

4. The flashlight _____ as I was _____ to my seat.

5. I have _____ a _____ from this movie on TV.

6. The _____ goes out at _____ to save the princess.

7. They _____ a boat and _____ on a horse.

8. They _____ a _____ of sheep following them.

9. After a _____ of running, they felt _____ .

10. At the end, _____ safe in _____ castle.

Grammar, Mechanics, and Usage Handbook and Glossary

This **Grammar, Mechanics, and Usage Handbook and Glossary** is a good reference for writers. It contains rules about capitalization and punctuation. It also contains some information about verb forms, adjective forms, and noun spellings. You'll find the U.S. Postal Service state abbreviations in this handbook, too.

Punctuation Guide

End Punctuation

Use end punctuation at the end of a sentence.

A *period* ends a declarative sentence. A declarative sentence makes a statement.

Jan rides a blue bike.

A *period* ends an imperative sentence. An imperative sentence makes a command or a request.

Clean your room. (command)
Please finish your lunch. (request)

A *question mark* ends an interrogative sentence. An interrogative sentence asks a question.

Where is the dog?

An *exclamation mark* ends an exclamatory sentence. An exclamatory sentence expresses strong emotion.

I scored a home run!

Periods

Use a *period* at the end of an abbreviation (in informal writing).

Street—St.   Route—Rte.   Saint—St.
Saturday—Sat.   November—Nov.
David Klein, M.D. (Medical Doctor)
Harold Brown, Sr. (Senior)

Use a *period* in abbreviations for time (in both formal and informal writing).

10:30 A.M.   2:15 P.M.

Use a *period* after initials.

K. Simpson   Linda F. Crane

Use a *period* after numerals and letters in outlines.

I. Craft projects
  A. Macrame
  B. Needlepoint

Commas

Use a *comma* between the name of a city and a state in an address.

Oklahoma City, Oklahoma   Bend, OR

Use a *comma* before and after the name of a state or a country when it is used with the name of a city in a sentence.

We will see St. Louis, Missouri, and Minneapolis, Minnesota, on our way to California.

Use a *comma* between the day and year in a date.

August 24, 1959

Use a *comma* before and after the year when it is used with both the month and the day in a sentence. Do not use a comma if only the month and the year are given.

I visited my aunt on June 30, 1982, at her summer cabin.
I visited my aunt in June 1982 at her summer cabin.

Use *commas* to separate three or more items in a series.

At camp we will swim, canoe, and sail.

Use a *comma* before *and, but,* or *or* when they join simple sentences to form a compound sentence.

Allen made pizza, and Alex made lemonade.

Use a *comma* after the greeting in a friendly letter and after the closing in all letters.

Dear Jamie,   Best wishes,

Use a *comma* to set off a direct quotation.

"My skates are new," bragged Joey.

"My sister will help us," said Carl, "after breakfast."

Colons

Use a *colon* to separate the hour and the minute when you write the time of day.

I have a piano lesson at 4:30 this afternoon.

Quotation Marks

Use *quotation marks* before and after a direct quotation, the exact words that a speaker says.

Darlene said, "I'll be back later."

Use a *comma* to separate a phrase such as *he said* from the quotation itself. Place the comma outside the opening quotation marks but inside the closing quotation marks.

"Class will begin," she said, "at the sound of the bell."

Place a *period* inside closing quotation marks.

Paul said, "I've never seen a red seashell."

Place a *question mark* or an *exclamation mark* inside the quotation marks when it is part of the quotation.

Bruce asked, "Do we have to go home now?"

Use *quotation marks* around the title of a short story, a song, a short poem, a magazine or newspaper article, and a chapter of a book.

Short Story: "Cinderella"

Song: "Oh, Susanna"

Poem: "Summer"

Magazine Article: "Parachuting"
Newspaper Article: "Living in Mexico"
Book Chapter: "Caring for Goldfish"

Italics (Underlining)

Use *italics* or *underlining* to set off the title of a book, film, magazine, or newspaper.

Little Women   *Gone With the Wind*   *Life*
San Diego Union

Apostrophes

Use an *apostrophe* and an *s* ('s) to form the possessive of a singular noun.

Carla's box   the cat's dish

Use an *apostrophe* and an *s* ('s) to form the possessive of a plural noun that does not end in *s*.

the women's club   the children's rooms

Use an *apostrophe* alone to form the possessive of a plural noun that ends in *s*.

the boys' chorus   the students' library

Use an *apostrophe* in a contraction to show where letters have been omitted.

she + is = she's   we + will = we'll   are + not = aren't

Hyphens

Use a *hyphen* to show the division of a word at the end of a line. Divide the word between syllables.

My class wants to go on a field trip to the sea-
shore this year.

Abbreviations

In both informal and formal writing you may use abbreviations for certain organizations and government agencies. Such abbreviations usually contain all capital letters and no periods.

United Nations (UN)

In informal writing and on envelopes, you may use U.S. Postal Service abbreviations for the names of states.

Alabama – AL	Kentucky – KY	Ohio – OH
Alaska – AK	Louisiana – LA	Oklahoma – OK
Arizona – AZ	Maine – ME	Oregon – OR
Arkansas – AR	Maryland – MD	Pennsylvania – PA
California – CA	Massachusetts – MA	Rhode Island – RI
Colorado – CO	Michigan – MI	South Carolina – SC
Connecticut – CT	Minnesota – MN	South Dakota – SD
Delaware – DE	Mississippi – MS	Tennessee – TN
District of	Missouri – MO	Texas – TX
Columbia – DC	Montana – MT	Utah – UT
Florida – FL	Nebraska – NE	Vermont – VT
Georgia – GA	Nevada – NV	Virginia – VA
Hawaii – HI	New Hampshire – NH	Washington – WA
Idaho – ID	New Jersey – NJ	West Virginia – WV
Illinois – IL	New Mexico – NM	Wisconsin – WI
Indiana – IN	New York – NY	Wyoming – WY
Iowa – IA	North Carolina – NC	
Kansas – KS	North Dakota – ND	

In scientific writing, use abbreviations for units of measure. The abbreviation is the same for singular and plural units.

inch–in.   pounds–lb   kilometer–km   liter–l

CAPITALIZATION GUIDE

First Words in Sentences _____

Capitalize the first word of a sentence.

Maria eats an apple.

Capitalize the first word of a direct quotation.
   Mrs. Singh called, "You may form teams for softball."

Capitalize all words in a letter's greeting.
   Dear Danny,

Capitalize the first word in the closing of a letter.
   Yours truly,

Proper Nouns: Names and Titles of People

Capitalize the names of people and the initials that stand for their names.
   Mary L. Carter   M. L. Carter

Capitalize titles of respect or abbreviations of titles when they come before the names of people.
   Mrs. Doris Clay   Captain L. E. Radner   Dr. Russell Freeman

Capitalize words that show family relationships when used as titles or as substitutes for a person's name.
   We will ask Mom and Aunt Sue to pick us up after the game.

Do not capitalize words that show family relationships when they follow a possessive noun or pronoun.
   Clark's father is a bus driver.
   His uncle works in the post office.

Capitalize the pronoun *I*.
   May I stay after school?

Proper Nouns: Names of Places

Capitalize the names of cities, states, countries, and continents.
   Omaha   Arizona   Panama   Europe

Capitalize the names of bodies of water and geographical features.
   Arctic Ocean   the Catskill Mountains

Capitalize the names of sections of the country.
the North   the Southeast

Do not capitalize words that are used just to show direction.
My cousin's camp is north of the lake.

Capitalize the names of streets and highways.
Canal Street   Highway 95

Capitalize the names of buildings and bridges.
Eiffel Tower   Triborough Bridge

Capitalize the names of stars and planets.
North Star   Mercury

Other Proper Nouns and Adjectives

Capitalize the names of schools, clubs, and businesses.
Valley Elementary School   Boy Scouts
National Oil Company

Capitalize the names of historic events, periods of time, and documents.
the Civil War   Middle Ages
the Declaration of Independence

Capitalize the days of the week, months of the year, and holidays. Do not capitalize the names of the seasons.
Wednesday   May   Labor Day   fall

Capitalize abbreviations.
Terrence Prine, Sr.   Tues.   Pvt. James Lane

Capitalize the first word and all important words in the titles of books, plays, short stories, poems, films, articles, newspapers, magazines, TV series, chapters of books, and songs.
Book: *Ramona*   Newspaper: *Chicago Tribune*
Play: *Cats*   Magazine: *Life*

Short Story: "Little Red Riding Hood"

Poem: "Winter"

Film: *The Little Mermaid*

Article: "The Homeless"

Book Chapter: "Puzzles and Games"

TV Series: *Doogie Howser*

Song: "Old Man River"

Capitalize the names of ethnic groups, nationalities, and languages.

Hispanic   Scottish   Spanish

Capitalize proper adjectives that are formed from the names of ethnic groups and nationalities.

Spanish olives   Colombian coffee

Capitalize the first word of each main topic and subtopic in an outline.

I. Garden vegetables
  A. Carrots
  B. Lettuce

Usage Guide

Forming Noun Plurals

You can use this chart when you want to spell plural nouns. Remember, some plural nouns have irregular spellings. Other plural nouns keep the same spelling as the singular form.

Singular Nouns	To Form Plural	Examples
most singular nouns	add *s*	girl dog hat girls dogs hats
nouns ending with *s, ss, x, z, ch, sh*	add *es*	box watch kiss boxes watches kisses

nouns ending with a consonant and *y*	change the *y* to *i* and add *es*	hobby city sky hobbies cities skies
some irregular nouns	change their spelling	tooth foot man teeth feet men
a few irregular nouns	keep the same spelling	moose deer trout

Verb Forms

Irregular verbs do not add *ed* or *d* to form the past or past participle.

Verb	Past	Past Participle
be	was, were	(have, has, or had) been
do	did	(have, has, or had) done
go	went	(have, has, or had) gone
begin	began	(have, has, or had) begun
sing	sang	(have, has, or had) sung
eat	ate	(have, has, or had) eaten
give	gave	(have, has, or had) given
grow	grew	(have, has, or had) grown
see	saw	(have, has, or had) seen

Adjective Forms

You can use this chart when you need help with comparative and superlative adjective forms. Remember, some adjectives are irregular. They do not form their comparative or superlative forms in the usual way.

Adjective	Compares Two Nouns	Compares More Than Two Nouns
small	smaller	smallest
thin	thinner	thinnest
lengthy	lengthier	lengthiest
tiny	tinier	tiniest

Glossary of Writing, Language, and Literary Terms

This *glossary* explains writing, language, and literary words and phrases that might be helpful to you in your writing. You might want to keep this glossary in your writing folder, too.

Writing Terms

audience — the reader or readers for whom something is written

brainstorming — a way to focus a writing topic by listing any thoughts that come to mind about the topic

charting — a way to organize and classify ideas and information by gathering them under different headings—especially useful in comparing and contrasting

checklist — a list of items, such as tasks or topic details, that can be used as an organizer and as a reference source. See also **listing**.

chronological order — the arrangement of events in the order in which they occur in time. See also **time order.**

clarity — the exactness with which the ideas and purpose of a piece of writing are expressed

clustering	a way to explore ideas by gathering details related to the specific writing topic
coherence	the orderly arrangement of ideas in a piece of writing
compare	to explain how two or more things are alike
conference	a meeting between the writer and a partner or a teacher, or in a group, to ask and answer questions about the writing in progress, with the purpose of improving it
contrast	to explain how two or more things are different
description	a piece of writing that creates a clear and vivid picture of a person, place, or thing
detail sentences	sentences that tell more about the main idea of a paragraph
diagram	a visual or graphic presentation of information; often used to organize information during prewriting. A Venn diagram is particularly useful for comparing and contrasting.
drafting	the act of capturing ideas on paper; a stage in the recursive process of writing during which the writer gets his or her basic ideas down on paper
elaboration	a writing strategy in which details and images are added to a piece of writing in order to give the topic fuller treatment

entertaining writing	a piece of writing, often humorous or suspenseful, that amuses, intrigues, diverts, or engages the reader for the particular purpose of entertainment
explanation	a piece of writing that presents the facts about a subject in a clear and logical way
freewriting	a way to generate ideas by simply writing continuously for a specified time, without stopping to elaborate or to correct errors
informative writing	a piece of writing that presents information to a reader in a clear, accurate, complete, and coherent way
instructions	an explanation or set of directions for how to do something. The steps in a set of instructions are arranged in a logical way, so that other people can repeat the activity.
letter	a way to communicate informally or formally with someone in writing. A friendly letter has five parts, each of which gives the person who receives the letter important information, and is personal in nature. A business letter has six parts and is written to an audience often unknown to the writer.
listing	a way to organize your thoughts by writing them down and putting them in order—possibly by numbering them
logical order	an arrangement of ideas in an order that makes sense and is easy for the reader to follow

outline	a way to organize topic-related ideas in the order in which they will be discussed—especially useful in organizing a research report
overall impression	the general idea or feeling expressed in a description
paragraph	a section of a written work, consisting of one or more sentences on a single subject or idea and beginning on a new and indented line
personal narrative	a piece of writing in which the writer tells about something that has happened in his or her life
persuasive writing	writing that encourages an audience to share the writer's beliefs, opinions, or point of view
prewriting	the stage in the writing process in which the writer chooses a topic, explores ideas, gathers information, and organizes his or her material before drafting
prewriting strategies	particular ways of gathering, exploring, planning, and organizing ideas before writing a first draft. See entries for individual prewriting strategies: **brainstorming, charting, clustering, freewriting, listing,** and **outlining**
proofreading	to review writing in order to correct errors in punctuation, capitalization, spelling, and grammar
publishing	to share written work with an audience—for example, by reading it aloud, contributing it to a school paper, or posting it on a bulletin board

purpose   the writer's reason for writing—for example, to explain, to entertain, or to persuade

reflective writing   a piece of writing in which the writer's personal thoughts, ideas, or feelings become an important part of the form. That form can be a poem, a story, or an essay, for example.

report   a piece of writing that provides information about a specific subject. A **book review** is a kind of report that gives information about a book the writer has read, as well as the writer's opinions about it. A **research report** summarizes information from many sources about a subject.

revising   to improve a draft by adding or taking out information, combining and reordering sentences, adding information, or changing word choice according to the purpose and audience

sensory details   in a description, the details that appeal to the reader's five senses—sight, sound, touch, taste, and smell

story chart   a way to gather ideas and details under headings important for the writing of a story

style   a writer's use of language and sentence structure to create a particular tone

summary   an account that tells the most important ideas of what has been read or observed by the writer. A summary can include

	information from one source or from multiple sources.
supporting details	facts, examples, or sensory details that give more information about the main idea of a paragraph
time line	a way to organize the events of a narrative in chronological order
time order	the arrangement of events in a composition according to when they occur in time— also called **chronological order.** Some time-order words are *first, next, then,* and *last.*
tone	the feeling or attitude a writer expresses toward the subject of a composition through his or her particular style of writing. For example, a writer's tone may be formal, informal, humorous, or critical.
topic sentence	the sentence that states the main idea of an informative, explanatory, or persuasive paragraph
transition words	words or phrases that may help writers to compare and contrast, such as *on one hand* and *on the other hand;* also, words that link sentences in a narrative, such as *finally* and *in the meantime*
voice	the quality of a piece of writing that makes it distinctively the writer's own
writing process	the recursive stages involved in writing, which usually include prewriting, writing

a draft, revising, proofreading, and publishing

Language Terms

action verb	a word that expresses action She *strolled* in the garden.
adjective	a word that modifies, or describes, a noun or pronoun She was the *smallest* person on the stage.
adjective phrase	a prepositional phrase that modifies, or describes, a noun or pronoun The tie *of blue silk* is in the window.
adverb	a word that modifies a verb, an adjective, or another adverb She sang *dreadfully.*
adverb phrase	a prepositional phrase that modifies, or describes, a verb, an adjective, or an adverb The man stands *to the right.*
antecedent	a word or group of words to which a pronoun refers *Mary* is a good player, but she tires easily.
appositive	a word or group of words that follows and identifies a noun The Mississippi, *a river in the United States,* is very long.
article	the special adjectives *a, an,* or *the* *The* girl gave *an* egg to *a* child.
common noun	a noun that names any person, place, or thing When will the *coach* arrive?

complete predicate   all the words that tell what the subject of a sentence does or is
> Sally *wrote a play for her class.*

complete subject   all the words that tell whom or what the sentence is about
> *Bread and cheese* are my favorite foods.

compound sentence   a sentence that contains two sentences joined by a comma and the words *and, or,* or *but*
> I love milk, and I drink it often.

conjunction   a word that joins other words or groups of words in a sentence
> Jan *and* Mark worked together.

demonstrative adjective   an adjective that points out something or describes a noun by answering the questions *which one?* or *which ones?*
> *That* student is the best in the class.

direct object   a noun or pronoun that receives the action of the verb
> Ed gave a *speech* to the class.

helping verb   a verb that helps the main verb to express action
> Lee *has* searched for the missing puzzle piece.

indefinite pronoun   a pronoun that does not refer to a particular person, place, or thing
> Does *anyone* have a book I can borrow?

indirect object   a noun or pronoun that answers the questions *to whom? for whom? to what?* or *for what?* after an action verb
> Sid gave *Sally* a job.

linking verb	a verb that connects the subject of a sentence to a noun or an adjective in the predicate Joan *is* captain of the team.
noun	a word that names a person, place, or thing The *player* pitched a *ball* at the *ball park*.
object of a preposition	a noun or a pronoun that follows the preposition in a prepositional phrase I won a prize at the *fair*.
object pronoun	a pronoun used as an object of the preposition, a direct object, or an indirect object Sarah gave *me* an apple.
possessive noun	a noun that shows ownership Are you *Ted's* cousin?
possessive pronoun	a pronoun that shows who or what owns something *Her* coat is blue.
predicate adjective	an adjective that follows a linking verb and describes the subject The boy is *tall*.
predicate noun	a noun that follows a linking verb and describes the subject Carl was the *secretary*.
preposition	a word that relates a noun or pronoun to another word in the sentence She gave me a box *of* cookies.

prepositional phrase a group of words that begins with a preposition and ends with a noun or pronoun
The glass *near the toaster* is mine.

pronoun a word that takes the place of one or more nouns and the words that go with the nouns
She gave *me* a book.

proper adjective an adjective formed from a proper noun
She bought a *Native American* basket.

proper noun a noun that names a particular person, place, or thing
The *Empire State Building* is magnificent.

run-on sentence two or more sentences that have been joined together incorrectly
I bought a cake yesterday it was chocolate.

sentence a group of words that expresses a complete thought
Dan ran the marathon yesterday.

sentence fragment a group of words that does not express a complete thought
Ran the marathon yesterday.

subject pronoun a pronoun that is used as the subject of a sentence
She likes baseball very much.

Literary Terms

alliteration the repetition of the same first letter or initial consonant sound in a series of words—for example, "He clasps the crag with crooked hands."

autobiography	the story of a person's life written by that person
biography	the story of a real person's life, written by someone else
character sketch	a long description of a character that tries to present a thorough and vivid portrait of the character
characters	the people (or animals) who participate in the action of a story or play
concrete poem	a poem whose shape suggests the subject of the poem
dialog	the conversations the characters have in a story or a play
fiction	written work that tells about imaginary characters and events. Works of fiction can include novels, plays, poems, short stories, science fiction, folk and fairy tales, myths, and fables.
figurative language	words used in unusual rather than in exact or expected ways, frequently in poetry. **Simile** and **metaphor** are two common forms of figurative language.
free verse	a poem that sounds like ordinary speech and has no regular rhythm or rhyme
haiku	a poem of three lines and usually seventeen syllables in which the poet frequently reflects on life or nature

hyperbole	the use of extreme exaggeration in speaking or writing, usually not meant to be taken seriously
idiom	an expression with a special meaning different from the literal meanings of the individual words that make up the expression—for example, "Time flies."
imagery	the use of word pictures—images—in writing, to make a description more vivid through especially precise or colorful language
limerick	an English verse form consisting of five lines that rhyme *a a b b a.* The third and fourth lines have two stresses, and the other lines have three stresses.
lyric poem	a fairly short poem expressing the personal mood, feeling, or reflections of a single speaker
lyrics	the words of a song
metaphor	a figure of speech in which a comparison is made without using the words *like* or *as*—for example, "The field was a green blanket."
meter	the regular pattern of beats in a poem
nonfiction	written work that deals with real situations, people, or events. Nonfiction works include biographies, autobiographies, articles, editorials, and news stories.
onomatopoeia	the formation of words and images in imitation of actual sounds—for example, "the *whizz* of the skates."

personification   a description in which human qualities are given to something that is not human—for example, "The leaves chased each other across the playground."

plot   the action or sequence of events in a story, novel, play, or narrative poem

proverb   a short, familiar saying that expresses a common truth or wise observation

repetition   the use of the same word, phrase, or sound more than once, for emphasis or effect, in a piece of writing

rhyme   the repetition of syllables that sound alike, especially at the ends of lines of poetry:
> The wrinkled sea beneath him crawls;
> He watches from his mountain walls,
> And like a thunderbolt he falls.

rhythm   a pattern of stressed and unstressed syllables, like a regular musical beat, especially in a poem or song:
> And hand in hand, on the edge of the sand,
> They danced by the light of the moon.

setting   the time and place in which the events of a story occur

simile   a figure of speech in which a comparison is made using the words *like* or *as*—for example, "The kite soared like a bird."

stanza   a group of lines in a poem that form a complete unit, like a paragraph in a piece of prose writing

story	a piece of writing that has a sequence of events, or **plot.** The people in the story, or the **characters,** move the action of the story along. The **setting** is where and when the story takes place.
tall tale	a story in which the characters are larger than life and able to perform extraordinary feats. Exaggeration is used in a tall tale.
tanka	a poem of five lines and usually thirty-one syllables (5, 7, 5, 7, 7), that frequently expresses the poet's reflections on a subject from life or nature
theme	the main idea or meaning of a complete piece of writing
tone	the total effect of the language, word choice, and sentence structure used by a writer to express a certain feeling or attitude toward the subject

WRITING MODELS

The Thinking Cap

*This writer
starts out right
away with an
exaggeration.*

Megan walked home from school. She felt bad. Her big sister was so smart that she could do her homework just by looking at it. Megan wasn't like that. She worked and worked, but she always did something wrong.

"Put on your thinking cap," said her sister.

"Put on your thinking cap," said her teacher.

"Put on your thinking cap," said her mother.

"I wish I *had* a thinking cap," said Megan sadly.

Just then, she saw something red in the bushes. She pulled it out. It was a little hat. She tried it on. It fit perfectly.

"What a nice day," Megan thought. "I guess that high pressure from the east warmed the air."

She stopped. She took off the hat and looked at it. Then she put it back on.

"I have gone 800 meters, and I have 500 meters left to go," she thought.

How strange! She hardly knew what a meter was!

Megan wore the hat home. Her mother was cooking.

"If you double that recipe, you'll need 3½ cups of flour," said Megan. Her mother dropped her spoon.

"May I help you with your homework?" Megan asked her sister. "I can act out all the parts in *Romeo and Juliet*." Her sister fainted.

*The problem
Megan had at
the beginning of
the story is
solved by the
end.*

Megan wore the hat to school the next day. In no time, her teacher saw that Megan should graduate right away and go to college. At graduation, most people wore black caps with tassels. Megan wore her red hat. She never took it off as long as she lived.

The Canoe Trip That Never Happened

FAST FOCUS

This writer makes it clear that he is the one telling the story.

Last summer, my dad decided that we should go canoeing on the Green River. He got very excited about it. My mom was kind of excited. I was pretty excited. My sister was disgusted. She hates camping, and she doesn't like canoeing.

We bought all kinds of stuff for the trip. We bought new life jackets, a new tent, and waterproof boxes to hold our food and supplies. Dad gave me the job of navigator. That meant that I was in charge of the maps and the compass. I had to know where we were all the time. If we got lost, it was my fault. That was a great job for me, because I like maps. For weeks before we left, I read all the maps and planned where we should stop at night. I measured the river on the map and found out where the rapids were. I made all kinds of lists. I was ready to go.

If something interests you, show that in interesting writing. Then your reader will be interested, too.

We drove into Kentucky and arrived at the Green River. Surprise! The river was brown and full of logs and garbage. It had rained in Kentucky for a week, and the river was flooding. Our careful plans were ruined. My sister was glad. We ended up staying at motels and visiting museums. It was okay, but it was not as much fun as a canoe trip would have been. Maybe next year we can try again. We might even leave my sister at home.

These facts help you understand the title of the story.

Description of a Place

This first sentence gives an overall impression of the place.

The writer moves in order from left to right in this description.

A Distant Planet

Through his viewer, the Captain could see the bare, ugly planet they called Zarko. On the left, he saw a desert with yellow sand and no trees. Next to that, he saw bricks and stones. That was all that was left of the city of Xog. Past that on the right, he noticed a large, brown lake. It looked like a big puddle of mud. There were no birds around it, and no grass grew. Everything was yellow, gray, or brown. It looked gloomy and lonely.

FAST FOCUS

Ms. Mitsuka: Artist

This writer asked careful questions about Ms. Mitsuka's art to learn certain things.

When you write an interview, keep your audience in mind. What will they want to know?

Ms. Mitsuka is an artist who uses real plants and flowers in her art. I talked to Ms. Mitsuka about flower arranging. I asked her why she only used a few flowers in each bowl. She said that her art comes from very long ago. Each flower or leaf has a special meaning. Some are tall, and some are short. Ms. Mitsuka tries to balance tall and short flowers.

She said, "I try to make a simple picture that is pleasing to the eye."

Ms. Mitsuka's art gave me a new way of looking at flowers. You can see her work in the art room today or tomorrow.

FAST FOCUS

How to Plan a Family Picnic

*The first
sentence
introduces the
topic.*

   You can have a good family picnic if you follow some simple steps. First, make sure that everyone likes the food on the menu. It's terrible to spend all that time cooking and find out that your cousins hate chicken and Aunt Margie can't eat corn. Second, give everyone a little job to do. If Uncle Harry is minding the babies, they won't stick their fingers in the pies all the time. Third, serve the food before everyone is too bored. It's better to eat cold beans than to break up a big fight. Last of all, make sure all the people at the picnic clean up after themselves. Follow these rules, and your family will have fun, eat well, and get along.

*This writer uses
clear, exact
details to tell
just how to have
a successful
picnic—and a
little humor to
make it
interesting.*

FAST FOCUS

Spring Thaw

Colorful language lets your reader "see" what you see.

This writer uses words that start with s to make you think about the sound of a stream in springtime.

The snow is melting
And the icicles drip
Into the stream.
The water is clear
And cold and swirling.
It hits the stones
With an icy slap.
It picks up speed
Near the silver birches
And it splashes
And sprays
As it runs
To see
Spring.

Friendly Letter

FAST FOCUS

20 Valley Road
Winooski, VT 05404 ← HEADING
March 14, 1993

*You can involve
your reader by
asking questions.*

Dear Jim, ← GREETING

    Do you have recycling yet in New Hampshire?
You definitely should try the kind we have! It works
very well. ← BODY

*This writer uses
words like
should* and
great *to win Jim
over to her side.*

    Every family gets a big, green box. We put newspapers,
cans, and glass bottles in the box. Then we put it out at
the curb, and a truck comes to pick it up. It's great!
Before, we had to go to the dump every week.

    I hope your family is well. Write me a letter!

*Notice that
Dahlia's letter is
in five parts.*

Your friend, ← CLOSING

Dahlia ← SIGNATURE

Character Sketch

This writer gives you an overall impression of Aunt Myrna in the first sentence.

Colorful, exact words help you "see" the person being described.

My Favorite Aunt

My Aunt Myrna makes me think of warm blankets, soft music, and gingersnaps. She is the cuddliest person in the world. That's because she is big and soft, and she likes to hug me. She tucks me in and tells me stories, and her voice sounds like a lullaby. When I kiss her soft brown cheek, I always smell gingersnaps. All in all, Aunt Myrna is the most comfortable person I know.

Science Report

FAST FOCUS

FAST FOCUS

WHAT IS A TORNADO?

This writer used an encyclopedia to make sure the information given is correct.

When you write about science, present facts clearly and check to make sure they are correct.

A tornado is a dark cloud that moves down from a cloud mass and heads toward the earth. If there is a lot of warm, damp air down near the ground, and it meets cold, dry air from above, this could cause a tornado. Usually tornadoes happen on very warm, humid days. Winds inside a tornado can spin up to 300 miles per hour. These winds can destroy buildings and anything else in their path.

Two Bad Ants

by Chris Van Allsburg

Everybody remembers *Jumanji*, that strange book by Chris Van Allsburg. His pictures are enough to give you nightmares! This book has great pictures, too. It is about a band of ants who go exploring. Two bad ants did not go home with the others. They stay and have adventures. Some of their adventures are very dangerous. At times, it looks like they will not survive! The pictures make things like faucets or coffee cups seem scary and weird. This is another wonderful book by Chris Van Allsburg. If you liked *Jumanji,* you'll like *Two Bad Ants*.

Our Neighbor's Government

This report is organized to show first how Canadian government is similar to and then how it is different from United States government.

A report should present facts clearly and understandably.

Canada is right next door, but it is not just like the United States. Some things about its government are like ours, but other things are different.

Like our Congress, the Canadian Parliament is divided into a Senate and a House. In both countries, House members are elected by the people. In the United States, the Senate members are also voted in by the people. In Canada, they are appointed to their jobs. In Canada, the prime minister is the head of the government, but the queen of England is the head of state. Unlike our President, the Canadian prime minister is a member of the House of Commons.

Invitation

Use friendly letter form to write an invitation.

Tell WHAT, WHEN, and WHERE the event is.

70 Elm Street ← HEADING
Hartford, CT 06143
June 21, 1995

Dear Sara, ← GREETING

   I would like you to come to my birthday ← BODY
party next Saturday, June 27. We will meet at my house
at 70 Elm Street at 1:00 P.M. and go to the zoo to see
the baby animals. I hope you can come. Please call me
at 277-0099 to let me know.

Your friend, ← CLOSING

Mariah ← SIGNATURE

Thank-You Letter

FAST FOCUS

Thank the reader, and tell why you are thanking him or her.

Use polite but friendly language in a thank-you letter.

628 Lake Road ← HEADING
Urbana, IL 81801
November 4, 1995

Dear Evan, ← GREETING

   Thank you for bringing that great video ← BODY
game for me to play while I was sick. I think it helped
me get better! It was really nice of you. I'll be back in
school next week, and I can't wait to see you and the
rest of the team.

Your friend, ← CLOSING

Jasper ← SIGNATURE

Business Letter

Stonewall School   ← HEADING
Weatherford, OK 73096
September 3, 1993

*A business
letter includes
the address of
the reader as
well as the
writer.*

Ms. Loretta Alvarez   ← INSIDE
Postal Rate Commission   ADDRESS
2000 L Street, NW
Washington, DC 20268

Dear Ms. Alvarez: ← GREETING

   Our class thinks that the amount we pay ← BODY
for stamps should not go up any more. Since we
started school, it has gone up 5¢. Writing letters is a
good way to learn, but we can't afford to send very
many. Do you have any ideas about how our class can
save money on postage?

   Thank you for your help.

*In this kind of
letter, use
polite, formal
language.*

Sincerely,   ← CLOSING

Room 304   ← SIGNATURE

*Sincerely is a
good closing for
this kind of
letter.*

Envelope

*The writer's
address goes on
the top left
corner.*

*The reader's
address goes in
the middle of
the envelope.*

Room 304
Stonewall School
Weatherford, OK 73096

      Ms. Loretta Alvarez
      Postal Rate Commission
      2000 L Street, NW
      Washington, DC 20268

Announcement

The writer has made plain WHEN and WHERE the event will take place.

An announcement should be neat and clear.

COME ONE, COME ALL

to the Seaside School

BAKE SALE

Pies, Cakes, Cookies, Brownies, Muffins

Friday, May 30

2:30 P.M. – 4:30 P.M.

in the Seaside School Gym

The money will be used to buy supplies for the art room.

Application

FAST FOCUS

Fill out an application completely and accurately.

Make sure to follow directions.

Dryden Library Card Application

1. Name _Monica Chang_

2. Address _235 Valley Road, Dryden, New York_

3. Home Phone _533-0800_

4. Age _8_

    If you are 12 years old or younger, please fill out item 5. If not, skip to item 6.

5. Name of Parent or Guardian _Alfred Chang_

    I promise to abide by the rules of the library.

6. Signature _Monica Chang_

Scene

FAST FOCUS

Cast of Characters

Carlitos, a Venezuelan boy
Camila, a Venezuelan girl

(*Carlitos and Camila are talking on the stoop of their building in the city.*)

Capital letters and colons (:) show who is speaking.

CARLITOS: The mayor will not let us have a playground.

CAMILA (*angrily*): That is not fair!

CARLITOS: Go find Cheo. We must think of a good plan.

The action is shown in parentheses.

CAMILA: Okay. (*She exits.*)

CARLITOS (*to himself*): We need a place to play. If the mayor won't help us, we must do it ourselves. (*He exits.*)

FAST FOCUS

PAUL SIMON: SUPERSTAR

This writer introduces the subject of the biography in the first sentence.

It makes sense to tell the story of a person's life in the order in which events happen.

Paul Simon was born in 1942 in Newark, New Jersey. Simon began to sing and write music as a teenager. He teamed up with his childhood friend Art Garfunkel to form the group Tom and Jerry, and the pair recorded a minor hit song while they were still in high school.

In the 1960s, under the name of Simon and Garfunkel, the group became one of the country's most popular singing teams. In 1965, they recorded Simon's folk song "Sounds of Silence" with a rock beat. Simon wrote most of the songs for the team including "Homeward Bound," which was recorded in 1966, and "Bridge Over Troubled Water," in 1970.

In 1970, Simon began his successful solo career. He has reunited in concert with Art Garfunkel from time to time and has also teamed up with other musicians from all over the world. He continues to write popular songs from his home in Montauk, New York, and people around the world look forward to his concerts.

Editorial

In an editorial, you state a definite point of view and try to convince the reader that you are right.

This writer includes facts to back up her opinions.

The middle school should have boy cheerleaders as well as girls. Right now, they only let girls on the squad. People like my brother, who is a great acrobat, can't even try out.

This is the nineties. Boys and girls are supposed to be equal. As a girl, I can try out for football, so why can't boys try out for cheerleading?

Many colleges have men cheerleaders. In fact, in the olden days, all cheerleaders were men.

When I get to middle school, I hope I can be a cheerleader alongside my friend Jen and my friend Alonzo. It's only fair!

Directions to a Place

Write directions in step-by-step order.

Include any important details that will help your reader.

It is easy to get to Yellow Barn State Forest from my house. Walk out the driveway and turn right onto Midline Road. Follow Midline Road for one-half mile. You will pass Hunt Hill Road on your left. When you see a house on your right with a blue roof, you are coming to Yellow Barn Road. Turn right onto Yellow Barn Road. The paved road turns into a dirt road very soon. Where the dirt road begins, a path goes off to the right. The sign there says, ''Yellow Barn State Forest.''

WRITING PROMPTS

Writing Prompt   Level 8

Unit 1: Story

In the book *Lon Po Po,* some clever children fool a wolf who wants to eat them. Have you ever been in a situation where you had to use brain power to get what you wanted? Have you ever used a clever trick to get out of danger? Write a story for a classmate about your own experience. Or, if you prefer, write about an imaginary character. As a prewriting technique, you might want to create a story map in which you list your story characters, the setting, some events in the story, and how the story ends. When you revise, you might want to check your story against your map to make sure you have not left out anything.

Writing Prompt

Unit 2: Description

"Opt: An Illusionary Tale" is a story about how people look at things. There are a lot of pictures in this selection. They show how people and objects can look different even when they are actually the same. Write a description about an object or a person that looks different depending on where you are when you look at it. For example, does writing on the chalkboard look the same up close as it does from five feet away? Does your friend look the same when you're standing eye-to-eye as when you're three feet apart? As a prewriting technique, you might want to make a list of the qualities that the object or person has when you see it up close, or in the dark, or in a special light. Then write about how it looks from far away, or in a different light.

Writing Prompt

Unit 3: How-To Guide

How My Parents Learned to Eat is a story about how an American sailor and a Japanese student learn about each other's lives. The American wants to find out how to eat with chopsticks. The Japanese student wants to learn how to use a knife and fork. Think of something that you know how to do well. Write a how-to guide explaining how you learned to do it. List all the steps in order. Write your guide for someone in the second grade. As a prewriting technique, you might want to create a flowchart of the steps involved in the process you are explaining. When you revise, close your eyes and visualize all the steps in the process to make sure you do not need to add anything.

Unit 1: Letter

In *The Great Kapok Tree,* all the creatures of the Amazon rain forest whisper in a sleeping man's ear. They don't want him to chop down the tree under which he's dozing. Each of them tells him what good the kapok tree brings to the forest. They persuade him to save the tree. Think of an issue that you feel strongly about. Perhaps it is an issue that has to do with animals or with the environment or the homeless. Write a letter to a public official expressing your view on the issue. Try to convince the public official to take action. As a prewriting technique, you might want to make a list of reasons to support your position. When you revise, you might want to check your letter against your list to make sure you do not need to add anything.

Writing Prompt

Unit 2: Report

In "Tornado Alert," readers find out how and why tornadoes happen. This selection gives a lot of information about different kinds of tornadoes. It also tells how fast they travel. Readers also learn what to do to avoid danger in a tornado. What kind of weather do you like best? What kind do you hate? Do some research about the kind of weather you choose, and write a report about it. Write a report for a friend. As a prewriting technique, you might want to make an outline. When you revise, you can check your report against the sections in your outline to make sure you have presented your report in a logical order.

Writing Prompt

Unit 3: Comparison/Contrast Composition

"Operation Rescue: Saving Sea Life from Oil Spills" tells about rescuing animals in danger. The article shows how veterinarians and zoo keepers help sea otters and seabirds in trouble. Each kind of animal needs help when it is harmed by an oil spill. Some of the help is the same for the animals and birds. Some of it is different. Writers often use comparison (pointing out likenesses) and contrast (pointing out differences) when they present information. Think of something you could compare and contrast. It might be something from science or nature, or it might be something from another subject area. Write a composition that compares and contrasts the two. Write your composition for your teacher. As a prewriting technique, you might want to make a VENN diagram to classify the likenesses or differences. When you revise, you might want to check your composition against your diagram to make sure you have put your likenesses and differences in the correct categories.

Writing Prompt with Picture Cue

Story

Look at this picture. Write a story based on what you see in it. Write your story for a friend. As a prewriting technique, you might want to use a story chart in which you outline setting, characters, and events. When you revise, you might want to close your eyes and imagine you see the major events in the story. Then look at what you have written to see if you need to tell more about any of the events.

Writing Prompt with Picture Cue

Description

What do you see in this picture? What are the children doing? Do they look happy or sad? How do the animals look? Are they peaceful? Write a description for a classmate. As a prewriting technique, you might want to create a cluster that presents the way everyone looks in the picture. When you revise, compare your story to your cluster to see if you have left out any details.

How-To Guide

Look at this picture. Imagine the steps that the builder went through to create the skateboard. What materials did he or she need? Write a how-to guide for building this skateboard. Write the guide for someone who is a few years younger than you are. As a prewriting technique, you might want to make a flowchart that lists the steps in order. When you revise, you might want to compare your draft against your flowchart to make sure that your steps are in order.

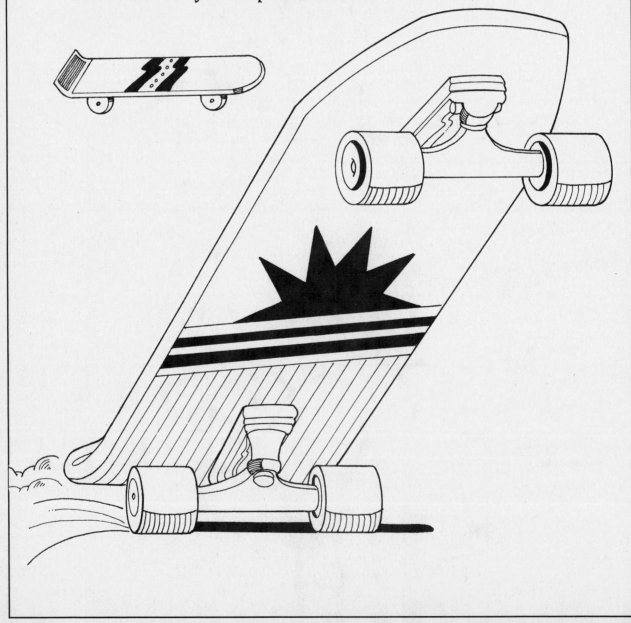

Writing Prompt with Picture Cue

Letter

What do you see in this picture? How do you think the otter feels? Write a letter to your local newspaper or school newspaper about the animal. In your letter try to persuade readers to help contribute to a fund to help save animals who have been harmed by an oil spill. As a prewriting technique, you might want to list the reasons why people should help. When you revise your letter, you might want to compare your draft to your original list to make sure you have given the most persuasive reasons.

Writing Prompt with Picture Cue

Comparison/Contrast Report

Look at this picture. In it are two birds. How are they alike? How are they different? Write a composition that compares and contrasts these birds. Write your composition for a relative. As a prewriting technique, you might want to make a chart to classify likenesses and differences. When you revise, you may wish to compare your draft to your chart to make sure that you have classified your details accurately.

Writing Prompt with Picture Cue

Comparison/Contrast Report

Look at this picture. In it are two pairs of headphones. How are they alike? How are they different? Write a composition that compares and contrasts these two headphones. Write your composition for a friend. As a prewriting technique, you might want to make a Venn diagram to classify likenesses and differences. When you revise, you may wish to compare your draft to your diagram to make sure that you have put your details into the correct categories.

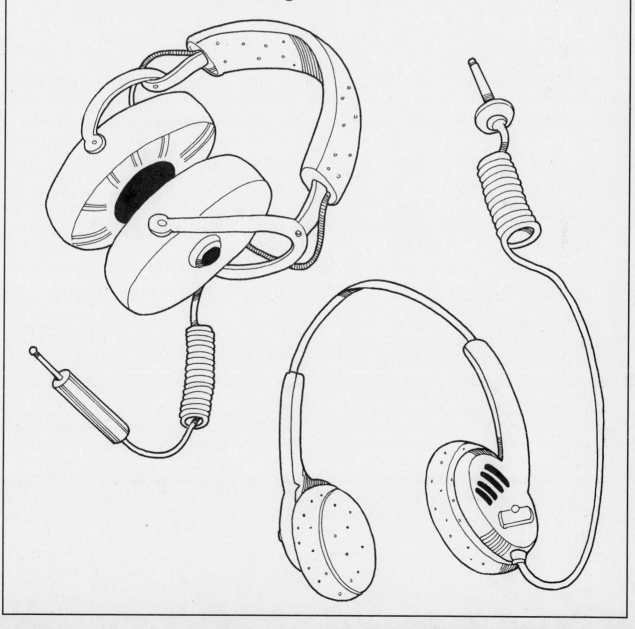

Spelling Strategies

Spelling Strategies and Tips

One of the most important things every writer does during the proofreading stage is to check that all of the words in a piece are correctly spelled. Poor spelling is more than an inconvenience to the reader. If even one or two words are spelled incorrectly, your writing may end up meaning something very different from what you wanted to say.

Try spelling difficult words syllable by syllable, saying the word quietly to yourself as you write it. If you pronounce it correctly, your chances of spelling it correctly are improved. Also, try to picture what the word looks like. This will almost always help you to find the correct spelling. Always check your dictionary for any spellings you aren't sure of.

Spelling rules can help you to spell certain kinds of words correctly. Remember—these rules are only hints to help you to develop a sense of what's correct and what isn't. English is a tricky language; the following rules almost always have exceptions, so you can't depend on them in every case.

Words with *ie* and *ei*	In most cases, a word is spelled with *ie* for the *e* sound, except when the *e* sound follows the letter *c:*
	   chief, relief, field, niece
	   receipt, ceiling, perceive
	In most cases, a word is spelled with *ei* when the sound is *not e,* especially if the sound is *a:*
	   eight, eighty, freight, neigh, sleigh
	Be careful, however! These are common exceptions to this rule:
	   friend, either, seize, weird

Adding *s* and *es*	In most cases, *s* can be added to a word without any other change in the spelling: pet/pets sign/signs lock/locks

If the word ends in *ch, s, sh, x,* or *z,* add *es:*

inch/inches   wish/wishes   buzz/buzzes

kiss/kisses   mix/mixes   chorus/choruses

For most nouns ending in a single *f,* change the *f* to *v* and add *es* to form the plural:

elf/elves   scarf/scarves   loaf/loaves

Here are some exceptions to this rule:

oaf/oafs   proof/proofs   chief/chiefs

Most words that end in *ff* simply add *s:*

cliff/cliffs   stuff/stuffs   sniff/sniffs

Words ending in *o*   Most words that end in a vowel followed by *o* add *s* to form the plural:

rodeo/rodeos   folio/folios   studio/studios

Most words that end in a consonant followed by *o* add *es* to form the plural:

hero/heroes   zero/zeroes   tomato/tomatoes

Some exceptions are words, mostly for musical terms, borrowed from the Italian language. Their plurals are usually formed simply by adding *s:*

piano/pianos   soprano/sopranos   cello/cellos

Sometimes, however, the original Italian plural form is used:

concerto/concerti   libretto/libretti

Adding *es, -ed,*   If a word ends in a consonant followed by *y,*
-*ing*, -*er*, and -*est*   change the *y* to *i* before adding any ending that does not begin with *i:*

ruby/rubies   rely/relies   carry/carried

For most words that end in a vowel followed by *y,* keep the *y* when adding an ending:

enjoy/enjoyed   stray/straying   obey/obeyed

Remember that some irregular verbs ignore this rule to form their past tenses:

say/said   buy/bought   pay/paid

In most cases, if a one-syllable word ends in one vowel and one consonant, the consonant doubles when an ending that begins with a vowel is added:

sag/sagged   trip/tripping   thin/thinnest

For most two-syllable words ending in one vowel and one consonant, the consonant doubles only if the accent falls on the second syllable:

trigger/triggered   bother/bothering

BUT: begin/beginning   prefer/preferred

If a word ends in a silent *e,* drop the *e* when adding an ending that begins with a vowel:

lose/loser   loose/loosest   shave/shaver

tape/taped   write/writing   breathe/breathing

Adding prefixes and suffixes

When you add a prefix to a word, the spelling of the base word usually stays the same:

tie/untie   behave/misbehave   arm/disarm

When you add a suffix, the spelling of the base word may change. If the base word ends in silent *e,* drop the *e* before a suffix that begins with a vowel:

operate/operator   type/typist   love/lovable

For most words ending in silent *e,* keep the *e* when adding a suffix that begins with a consonant:

love/loveless   shame/shameful   elope/elopement

When you add the suffix *-ness* or *-ly,* the spelling of the base word usually does not change:

strange/strangely   fine/fineness   quick/quickly

Common exceptions are adjectives ending in a single consonant following a vowel:

successful/successfully   metric/metrically

Other exceptions are certain one-syllable words ending in two vowels or a vowel and *y:*

true/truly   due/duly   gay/gaily

If a word ends in *y* and has more than one syllable, change the *y* to *i* before adding *-ness* or *-ly:*

happy/happily/happiness   crazy/crazily/craziness

Homophones

Homophones—words with different meanings and spellings that sound alike—are responsible for a great many misspellings. Be sure you know the *meaning* of the homophone you want to use. That will usually help you to spell it correctly. Here are a few of those most often misspelled and misused:

rain/rein/reign	pore/pour	sheer/shear
chilly/chili/Chile	flare/flair	bough/bow
pair/pear/pare	forth/fourth	higher/hire
close/clothes	to/too/two	lose/loose
piece/peace/peas	hours/ours	real/reel
through/threw	accept/except	so/sew/sow
stationary/stationery	principal/principle	

As was pointed out at the beginning of this section, rules of spelling won't be enough to help to you spell correctly in every case. There are many words in the English language whose spellings seem to obey no rules at all, or to contradict the rules you've taken so much trouble to learn. Some of them *do* follow the rules but are tricky to spell anyway. The only way to spell these "problem" words correctly every time is to memorize them.

To help you to do this, we've picked out some of the words that seem to give the most people most trouble most often—the words that you will see most frequently misspelled. Use this list or your dictionary often, whenever you are unsure of a word. The more often you see a word's correct spelling, the more likely you are to remember it for your own future use.

able	bathe	caught	dear
above	beautiful	cheese	decide
address	because	chief	dictionary
afraid	become	children	does
again	begin	close	done
ahead	behind	cloth	dozen
alley	believe	clothes	drawer
along	bottle	color	
already	bought	cough	early
always	breakfast	course	earn
another	breathe	cousin	engine
answer	brother	cover	enough
around	brought		every
aunt	build	daily	except
awake	busy	daughter	
awful	buy	dead	

famous
fare
favorite
feather
fence
finish
fire
forget
forty
fourth
fresh
friend
frighten
front
fruit

garage
garden
giant
glove
goes
gone
grammar
growl
grown
guess
guest

half
happen
heard

height
here
hour
huge
hundred
hungry

instead
iron
island

juice

knee
know

ladder
language
large
library
lightning
listen
lose

matter
maybe
meant
middle
minute
money
month
morning

nature
neighbor
nickel
niece
nineteen
ninety
ninth
none
nothing
number

ocean
often
once
only
oven

parade
paste
pear
people
please
poem
prayer
present
probably
promise
proud

quiet

receive
remember
rhyme

safety
said
sandwich
says
school
scratch
sense
seventy
sew
share
silence
similar
sincerely
sixth
smooth
soldier
some
sorry
special
stretch
strong
sudden
sugar
sure
surprise
sword

taken	tied	until	where
taught	tired	use	wire
tear	together	usual	without
tenth	tomorrow		woman
their	trouble	visit	women
thousand	truly		
thread	tunnel	wagon	your
threw	twenty	welcome	
through		were	

CUMULATIVE WORD LIST

able	bladder	check	draw
act	blink	chick	drew
afraid	bloom	chief	drift
afternoon	blue jay	child	
again	body	clapped	eagle
age	boot	classroom	early
alarm	brain	close	earn
alone	brand	cloud	earth
along	bread	coast	edge
angry	break	cold	egret
annoy	bright	cost	empty
ants	bring	count	enjoy
apart	broke	course	everywhere
author	built	cover	
awake	bunch	crawl	face
	bushes	creak	fact
badge	butter	creek	fade
band	butterfly	cricket	faraway
baseball	buzzard	crowd	feel
basket		cube	few
basketball	cage	cute	fight
became	calf		find
because	camp	dance	first
bedroom	candle	dark	flag
beetle	can't	dead	flash
beg	cardinal	didn't	flew
began	cause	dirty	flipped
behind	certain	doesn't	float
beside	chance	dose	flow
between	charge	dough	football
bigger	charm	dragonfly	forget

fork	high	kept	made
forth	highway	key	magic
fruit	hillside	kidney	mallard
furry	himself	kill	march
	hold	kind	mark
gas	homework	king	mask
gift	hook	kiss	maybe
give	hornet	knobby	mean
glade	horrible		middle
glands	hour	lady	might
goose	howl	ladybug	mile
grade	hug	lake	mind
grain	huge	later	minute
grasshopper	hum	lazy	mirror
great	hunch	lean	monkey
ground	hurry	learn	month
group		left	moth
growl	I'm	letter	mouth
	inside	life	mount
half	intestines	lift	munch
hand	island	light	
handful	isn't	line	near
happen	itself	liver	neck
hard	I've	living	neighbor
hatch		loon	noise
hawk	jar	loved	noon
hear	jaw	lumpy	notebook
heart	jeans	lunch	
hello	job	lung	odd
heron	join		oil
herself	juice		once
	jump		

osprey	prickly	scratch	smoke
ourselves	prince	scratchy	smooth
outside	purr	sea gull	soap
owl	push	search	soccer
own		second	soft
	queen	seem	soil
page	quick	sell	someone
pain	quilt	serve	something
paint		shade	sometimes
pants	race	shame	somewhere
paper	rails	sharp	sounds
park	rainbow	shells	soup
patches	rattle	shine	space
pelican	raven	shiny	sparrow
pen	real	shock	spell
penny	remember	shook	splash
person	rest	shout	spoonful
pillow	rib	side	sports
pine	right	sidewalk	sprawl
plain	ripe	sight	spring
plan	rising	sign	squirrel
plate	roach	signal	stairs
plow	roar	silky	stamp
point	robin	sitting	star
poison	rode	skin	step
poke	root	slept	sticky
pool	rope	slice	stomach
pop	rough	slip	storm
pounding		small	strange
pour	sail	smell	string
	schoolhouse	smile	strip

strong
sugar
supper
swipe

table
tape
taste
taught
teal
tennis
tern
terrible
test
themselves
thief
though
throat
throb

through
throw
thrush
thud
tight
tilt
tiny
tip
together
tonight
tooth
toys
track
trade
travel
truth
trying
turn

upon

wait
wall
warn
wasp
weather
weigh
whether
whipped
whistle
wild
wind
window
wing
wink
won
wonder
won't

wood duck
word
world
worry
worse
wound
wounded
wrap
wreck
wren

yellow jacket
you
you're
yourself
you've